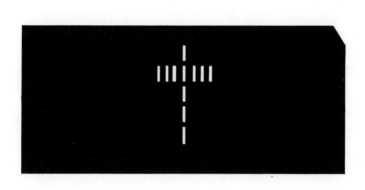

alba house DIVISION OF THE SOCIETY OF ST. PAUL   STATEN ISLAND, N. Y. 10314

A
"Non-Religious" Christianity?

Gustave Thils

Originally published under the title *Christianisme sans Religion?* by Editions Casterman — Tournai, Belgium.

Translated by John A. Otto, Ph.D.

200
T442c-T

Nihil Obstat:
  Daniel V. Flynn, J.C.D.
  Censor Librorum

Imprimatur:
  Joseph O'Brien, S.T.D., V.G.
  Archdiocese of New York
  March 24, 1970

The nihil obstat and imprimatur are official declarations that a book or pamphlet is free of doctrinal or moral error. No implication is contained therein that those who have granted the nihil obstat and imprimatur agree with the contents, opinions or statements expressed.

Library of Congress Catalog Card Number: 78-129171
SBN: 8189-0182-9

72- 345

PREFACE

We live in a world that is becoming more and more secularized. It is a world, and an age, in which the relationship (or, as some would have it, the opposition) of Christianity to religion has kindled much discussion. This book is dedicated to the exploration of this theme.

As for this work of Gustave Thils, undoubtedly one of its merits lies in the substantive accounts of authors who have investigated and analyzed the subject most thoroughly. Even though it cannot take the place of the authors themselves, it does provide the reader with direct access to their basic ideas through the numerous and copious citations found throughout the study.

But this is more than a compilation. Indeed, perhaps its foremost distinction is the critical effort, the weighing and sifting of what has been gathered. To the tempting appeal for a "religionless Christianity" the author applies the test of the Catholic faith, its essential statements on the relevance of the Word of God to human realities and the manifold relation of the Church to the world. He had been the first to attempt a "theology of earthly realities," and as such was particularly qualified to deal with the larger question of Christianity versus religion. As one would expect, he leans heavily on Vatican II, making generous use of the Constitution *Gaudium et Spes* (The Church in the Modern World) and all but as much of *Lumen Gentium* (On the Church).

Gustave Thils surveys his subject with a kind of synoptic eye, well-disciplined and well-balanced. This helps him escape certain pitfalls and temptations. He is not, for example, interested in exploitation for publicity's sake, as is sometimes the case in the treatment of topics that have become fashionable. And he has no ax to grind. Nor does he flounder in the con-

fusion and turmoil of ideas that marks much of the current debate in which he is participating — confusion reminiscent, at
times, of the punishment of Babel. This is not to imply that he
has said the last word on the important and complex problems
arising from the steady drift toward "secularization" and, more
generally, from the enormous changes we see taking place all
around. But it is to say that his study will help the reader to
discuss and explore them with better knowledge of the causes
and from the vantage ground of clearly-established positions.

René Marlé

TABLE OF CONTENTS

PREFACE   V

INTRODUCTION   XI

Part One

THE UNREST AND ITS ORIGINS

I. *The Abolition of Religions*   3

    Religion   4

    Revelation and Faith   10

    The Church   15

II. *The Emptiness of Religions*   21

    The Pastoral Problem   22

    Repudiation of "Religion"   24

    Christian Existence   28

III. *A "Secular" Religion*   31

    The Church in the Secular City   33

    God in the Secular City   41

IV. *The Era of Desacralization*   47

    The Central Theme of Desacralization   47

    "Sacral" vs "Secular" Image of the World   51

    The "Sacred"   57

Part Two

HORIZONS OF FAITH

I. *The Word of God and Man's Acceptance*   67

    The Word of God   67

    Acceptance of the Word   70

    Understanding of the Word   76

II. *Christian Faith and Christian Religion*   83

    Content of the Christian Message   83

Sacred Realities and Means of Sanctification   87

III. *Revelation and Active Presence in the World*   95

    The Problem   96

    Replies and Comments   99

Part Three

AGREEMENTS AND RESERVATIONS

I. *Karl Barth*   111

    Religion   111

    Faith   114

    The Church   116

II. *Dietrich Bonhoeffer*   119

    An Adult World   119

    Religionless Christianity   124

III. *Harvey Cox*   133

    The Secular City   133

X   A "Non-Religious" Christianity?

An Important Afterword   139

IV. *"Desacralization" and "Secularity"*   143

"Desacralization"   143

"Secularity"   149

CONCLUSION   159

INTRODUCTION

"Faith without religion," "religionless Christianity," "non-religious interpretation of christian revelation": expressions, these, which in some circles are very popular today and which (as well as others of the sort) the reader has doubtless met in print or conversation. Paradoxical and provocative, they attract and captivate not a few individuals. They admit of a variety of interpretations, well-suited to a variety of tastes, and this too seems a factor in their popularity.

Yet if this were all there was to it, that many people find these expressions, or the suggestions they convey, interesting and stimulating, it would be relatively easy to work out an accomodation. A few corrections here and there would suffice. Not that this would clear up all difficulties, but it could be enough to clear the air and to come face to face with the heart of the problem and the main thrust of the movement in question. But the fact of the matter is that the various interpretations mentioned a moment ago are not just innocent intellectual caperings. They become springboards for action, determining the conduct of individuals and even of the pastoral ministry. The result is chaos and confusion, in thought and action.

The easiest way, of course, to deal with these slogans and the theological positions behind them is simply to ignore them — pretend they don't exist, or if they do that they have nothing worthwhile to show for themselves. But the fact is they have met with considerable success, and the success is not all due to astute utilization of the means of communication, written or spoken. Nor are only those of meager culture, only "those who don't know better," attracted. The more realistic assessment is that they contain an element of truth, however difficult it may be to determine, and that this is at least partly the reason for their wide appeal. The element of truth, which appears in slogans generally, often consists of a promise of progress, or a foreboding sooner or later confirmed. In the interest of truth, therefore, we shall try to exercise caution as we move through this study, so that what appears sound and productive is not pruned off with what is found unhealthy and harmful.

What is currently referred to as the opposition between Christian faith and religion assumes various forms. It is not the same thing in Karl Barth as it is, say, in Dietrich Bonhoeffer or Harvey Cox, not to mention the representatives of "desacralization" and "secularity." In every case, therefore, it needs to be determined what these authors mean by "christian faith," what they have in mind when they speak of "religion," and what precisely they understand by "sacred." It is an arduous, wearisome task. And it is not always crowned with success. In fact, sometimes what seems success turns out to have been a will-of-the-wisp, a delusion.

In this limited study, however, it is obviously impossible to delve into every aspect of (for want of a better term) a movement that still gives no signs of having crystallized, that is still very much in the making and has yet to achieve a measure of integration as compared with its polymorphous character at the moment. All that can be expected, and all that we attempted, is to throw some light on the subject, focusing attention on certain aspects and attitudes of the movement with a view to exorcising it of its idols, the excesses and abuses that do sometimes appear. We were also very much concerned with cautioning the reader not to be misled by the paradoxical utterances that get the headlines and create a sensation. At the same time we would not have him lose sight of what is good, the valuable aspects of the movement, especially the appeal for a deeper understanding of Christianity and a constant effort toward renewal.

We said "valuable" aspects. And designedly. When Pope Paul VI received the members of the Concilium for the Implementation of the Constitution on the Liturgy (April 19, 1967), he noted with sorrow that there was a growing tendency to "desacralize" — *sacra indole exuere* — the liturgy, which he deplored all the more that such a development "necessarily involves the disintegration of religion itself." Yet the Holy Father hastened to add that "we are not unaware that any undertaking or doctrine that succeeds in sustaining and disseminating itself may contain a not negligible portion of truth — *non tenuem partem veritatis posse continere* — and that the promoters of new ideas may indeed be men of quality and learning. We for our part are always ready to give consideration to the positive aspects of any development pertaining to the ecclesial order." [1]

---

1. Latin text in *L'Osservatore Romano,* April 20, 1967, p. 1.

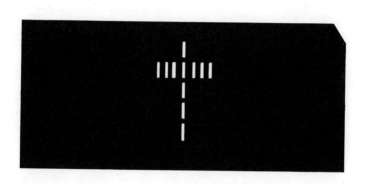

PART ONE

The Unrest and Its Origins

To promise an exposition of the contemporary religious unrest and its origins seems, no doubt, pretentious, nay presumptuous. For, certainly, the whys and wherefores of the present situation are multitudinous, and it would be literally impossible to deal with all of them in one small volume. On the other hand, it should be possible to give a general account of the theological positions which today are the principal inspiration for this movement that promotes the idea of opposition or incompatibility between christian faith and religion. Karl Barth[1] contends that the christian revelation is the abolition of religion. Dietrich Bonhoeffer presents the case for a-religious Christianity. In the United States Harvey Cox has come forward with the concept of a "secular" religion for the new Christianity. Add to these a large group of authors who urge de-sacralization in the name of the christian gospel. All in all, what we intend is a reasonably adequate and accurate delineation of the over-all movement as it emerges from these foremost representatives. A modest task — yet to accomplish it is already to have stunted, in some degree, the harm the movement may threaten as well as to have fostered the good it promises.

---

1. Karl Barth died Dec. 10, 1968, subsequent to the French edition of this work. He was 82, and had attained a theological eminence that was unique in our day. History may or may not make prophets of those who have hailed him as another Augustine or Aquinas, another Luther or Calvin. But history cannot but record that he towered above his colleagues in the field of Protestant theology and that the theological fraternity in general, Protestant or not, held him in esteem such as few men enjoy from their fellows. — [Tr.]

I

The Abolition of Religions

Not infrequently the criticism or depreciation of "religion" to the advantage of "faith" is inspired by Karl Barth's assertion that "the revelation of God is the abolition of religion." Whether Barth is right depends, obviously, on what is here meant by "religion." It is a question that has not gone begging, for there have been many attempts to find a clear answer.

In Protestant theology of the 20th century Karl Barth stands out as the man who broke with liberal "humanistic" Protestantism, to become something of a new prophet of the Word of God revealed in the Incarnation. Among Protestant theologians of the 19th century were those who reduced Christianity to a spiritual experience of purely human dimensions, albeit an experience of the highest sort, humanly speaking. Among them was Schleiermacher, who in 1799 wrote the famous *Discourse on Religion,* addressing it "to those of his scorners who could claim a cultivated mind." [1] The religion he proposed was, in the words of one critic, "a faith so watered down and attenuated that the result was an amalgam consisting in part of Fichtean and Schellingian idealism as transmitted through Kant, and in part of the estheticizing mystique of the (then) new school of poetry." [2]

If this was "religion," or if religion was born of such elements, it is fairly obvious why some Protestant thinkers rose up against it, in the name of revelation. Karl Barth was one of them, and his efforts did not go unnoticed or unappreciated. A professor of theology at the University of Geneva paid him this tribute: "I am

---

1. Quoted from the French translation, Paris, Aubier, 1944.
2. *Loc. cit.,* Introduction by I. J. Rouge, p. 5.

poles apart from the dogmatic teaching of Karl Barth, but I must acknowledge that this man has brought home to us the real meaning of the living Word of God." [3]

Religion

The first volume of Barth's *Church Dogmatics* contains a famous section titled "Revelation As the 'Assumption' of Religion." [4] According to the commentator "assumption" translates *Aufhebung*, which admits of such disparate meanings as "elevate," "abolish," "cover," "remove." Accordingly, religion in the Barthian sense is in some way assumed, suppressed, and replaced by revelation.

But how does revelation pertain to religion? Or, to put it differently, what is the "christian" meaning of religion? The question is Barth's, a question, he says, that must be faced.

The revelation of God by the Holy Spirit is real and possible as a determination of man's existence. If we deny this, how can we think of it as a revelation? But if we do not deny it, we have to recognize that it has at least the aspect and character of a human phenomenon. It is something which may be grasped historically and psychologically .... But the sphere to which this problem introduces us is the sphere of religion (p. 281).

In other words, there is both revelation and religion. But how are they related? How do they stand to each other? That is the real question.

What we think we know of the nature and incidence of religion must serve as a norm and principle by which to explain the

---

3. M. Dominicé, "Plaidoyer pour la liturgie," in *Hommage et Reconnaissance* (Neuchâtel, 1946), p. 187.
4. *Church Dogmatics*, vol. I, part 2; trans. by G. T. Thomson and Harold Knight (Edinburgh, T & T Clark, 1956), pp. 280-325. In the following pages, the page number in parentheses occurring in the text refer to this translation.

revelation of God; or, vice versa, . . . [do] we have to interpret the christian religion and all other religions by what we are told by God's revelation (p. 284)?

To this day, says Barth, modernistic Protestantism has made religion the basis for understanding and explaining revelation; which is not only alarming but heretical as well (p. 291). The theological position which he blames for this is clearly identified and described in a long note of some seven pages, so that he leaves no doubt that what he is reproaching is a specific school of religion, viz. that of liberal Protestantism (pp. 284-291).

But Barth's criticism is not limited to Protestantism. It embraces all religion. Revelation, he declares, enjoys complete superiority over religion. Revelation is not respected as it should be unless we consult it, and it alone, for the first and last word on religion (p. 295). Whence it follows that the theological problem of religion is not how to reconcile or harmonize the teachings of revelation and religion but "how to judge and evaluate, in the light of revelation and faith, whatever passes for religion among men" (pp. 296-297).

What this judgment will be can be gathered from the title to the present chapter. Revelation, in effect, assumes and replaces religion. It is its *Aufhebung,* its abolition. If this statement comes like a bolt out of the blue, Barth not only reaffirms it but goes even further. For his thesis, the point he is chiefly concerned to make, is that religion is "unbelief," *Unglaube* (p. 299). But why? and in what sense? Two reasons are given.

The first has to do with the truth and the knowledge of God. Revelation, in essence, is the act by which God permits himself to be known; man is taught something totally "new." Yet man tries to know God by himself, his own efforts. In this he is the victim of his religious condition, since the attempt is prompted by his religious attitude, yet is in conflict with the meaning and intent of revelation. However, the genuine believer, one who accepts revelation, with all its implications, can detect his error.

The genuine believer will not say that he came to faith from faith, but — from unbelief, even though the attitude and activity with which he met revelation, and still meets it, is religion .... From the standpoint of revelation religion is clearly seen to be a human attempt to anticipate what God in his revelation wills to do and does do. It is the attempted replacement of the divine work by a human manufacture. The divine reality offered and manifested to us in revelation is replaced by a concept of God arbitrarily and wilfully evolved by man (p. 302).

What Barth is saying is that revelation and religion are irreducibly opposed. And the opposition appears even more clearly when we stop to consider that revelation not only means that God makes himself known but that it is also a gratuitous act by which God reconciles man to himself. For it is in Jesus Christ, and in him alone, that we are converted, sanctified, saved. To believe in Jesus Christ is to acknowledge that such is the case, absolutely. Yet when we go to religion, what do we find? Man attempting to "finger God," "to corral for his own advantage" the forces and necessities of the universe, and even "to work his own justification and sanctification" (pp. 308, 309).

Where we want what is wanted in religion, i.e., justification and sanctification as our own work, we do not find ourselves . . . on the direct way to God . . . . On the contrary, we lock the door against God, we alienate ourselves from Him, we come into direct opposition to Him. God in His revelation will not allow man to try to come to terms with life, to justify and sanctify himself (p. 309).

Revelation, then, teaches us that God alone can make himself known, that he alone saves us. Revelation, in consequence, "shows up" religion — all religion — for what it actually is, an "unbelief"; for nothing is more contrary to faith than religion, nothing closer to idolatry, because in putting his trust in human

creatures man puts himself in the hands of idols and false gods
(p. 314).

And yet, Barth does speak of a "true religion." He keeps
the term and the notion, and uses it for the heading of a long
chapter (pp. 325-361). But the question is whether he keeps
the reality. The answer again involves the term *Aufhebung,*
which is explained more fully in this context than anywhere else.

No religion, says Barth, is true "in itself." To say that a
religion is true in itself is just as inconceivable as to say that
anyone is "just and good" in himself. True religion is like the
justified man; it is the work of grace. And grace, which is
capable of raising the dead and leading sinners to repentance,

> is just as much capable of creating, within the immense domain
> of false expressions of religion, a religion that is true (p. 326).

When Barth declares that religion is "assumed" by revelation,
this does not mean that it is simply denied or that it must be
considered as pure idolatry. Religion, he explains, is not only
assumed and borne by revelation but may also be justified and
sanctified by it.

> Revelation can adopt religion and mark it off as true religion.
> And it not only can. How do we come to assert that it can,
> if it has not already done so? There is a true religion: just
> as there are justified sinners. If we abide strictly by that ana-
> logy — and we are dealing not merely with an analogy, but
> in a comprehensive sense with the thing itself — we need have
> no hesitation in saying that the christian religion is the true
> religion (p. 326).

This passage clarifies Barth's position in regard to religion,
whatever its form. But the christian religion is, if the term be
allowed, in a privileged position because it knows the "judgment
of revelation." If by this judgment it stands accused and con-

victed of unbelief, that does not rule out the possibility of its
being re-created by grace (cf. pp. 354, 356). A true religion,
then, does exist in the world, namely the christian community
or the Church of God. This is the true religion in so far as
this community or Church lives by grace, *through the grace of
God.* "That is what makes [Christians] what they are. That is
what makes their religion true" (p. 345). The name of Jesus
Christ "creates" the christian religion.

> Apart from the act of its creation by the name of Jesus Christ,
> which like creation generally is a *creatio continua,* and there-
> fore apart from [its] creator, [the christian religion] has no
> reality (p. 346).

But the relation that exists between the name of Jesus Christ
and the christian religion stems also from an act of divine *election.*

> The christian religion did not possess any reality of its own.
> Considered in and for itself it never can. It is a mere possi-
> bility among a host of others (p. 348).

But the parallel with creation does not stop there, for

> as there is a *creatio continua* so also there is an *electio con-
> tinua,* better described . . . as God's faithfulness and patience
> [scil. with Christianity] (p. 349).

To be sure, we can point to profession of faith, to sacraments
and even to a theology. But if these things are "christian," it is
only because they are grace, and Barth means "pure grace,"
absolutely and exclusively. Indeed, that is what "christian" con-
notes, for this designation, which is so essential because through
it we express the name of Jesus Christ, never intends that "we
ourselves possess anything" (p. 349).
   The relationship between the name of Jesus Christ and the

christian religion derives also from an act of divine *justification,* i.e., from the divine forgiveness of sin. We must never forget that

> as far as the judgment of revelation is concerned, *all* religions are seen as manifestations of idolatry and self-justice. Christianity is no exception (p. 352).

If Christianity is just and good and true, it is through God's judgment and justice, through

> the union of the eternal Word of God with human nature, which, by this very union, is re-established in its original integrity, despite its basic pervertedness (p. 355).

In this connection Barth draws a comparison that throws further light on his thought.

> That the sun lights up this part of the earth and not that means for the earth no less than this, that day rules in the one part and night in the other. Yet the earth is the same in both places. In neither place is there anything in the earth itself to dispose it for the day. Apart from the sun it would everywhere be enwrapped in eternal night. The fact that it is partly in the day does not derive in any sense from the nature of the particular part as such. Now it is in exactly the same way that the light of the righteousness and judgment of God falls upon the world of man's religion, upon one part of that world, upon the christian religion, so that that religion is not in the night but in the day, it is not perverted but straight, it is not false religion but true (p. 353).

But let no one conclude, warns Barth, that this decisive fact of history was arbitrarily chosen. On the contrary, it is simply a consequence of God's justice and judgment. Hence, all is in order because what we are faced with here is the order willed by God, the unfathomable mystery of God's free choice.

Finally, the relationship between the name of Jesus Christ and the christian religion results also from an act of divine *sanctification*. In other words, the aforesaid justification produces a definite effect upon the christian religion, something of positive value. Barth explains it in words of the Incarnation.

> There is an event on God's side — which is the side of the incarnate Word of God — God adopting man and giving Himself to him. And corresponding to it there is a very definite event on man's side. This event is determined by the Word of God. It has its being and form in the world of human religion. But it is different from everything else in this sphere and having this form. The correspondence of the two events is the relationship between the name Jesus Christ and the christian religion from the standpoint of its sanctification (p. 358).

This being and this form have "no importance" of their own; their sole function is to bear witness to Jesus Christ, to be signs of the divine fact indicated by this name. In short, the christian religion is the "sacramental locus" created by the Holy Spirit as the frame within which God never ceases to speak to us through the signs of his revelation. It is also the "existence" of human beings who hear this God speak to them in his revelation.

Revelation and Faith

Two questions arise. What is this "revelation" that purifies? And, more important still, what is this act of "faith" that absorbs (so to speak) all religion?

The Holy Spirit himself, says Barth, vouches to the human spirit the work of the Holy Spirit in its behalf and thereby disposes the inward man for revelation. Man, in consequence, permits himself to be reconciled to God.[5] Faith has then been born in man and with it a living relationship between the believer and Christ. Faith lives from its Object (*Gegenstand*), more than that, has its source and foundation in this Object, which is to say in Christ giving himself to us as Object. What, then, is faith, or rather the act of faith? Entirely and exclusively the work or act of God.

Yet in this process of faith some human elements do somehow come into play. What is their role? The answer to this question will also make for further understanding of the faith-vs-religion issue.

For one thing, and strange as it may seem, the strict act of faith, precisely as *believing* act, is in no respect the doing of the person who makes it, namely the act of faith. Barth is very clear and precise on this point, as in the section of the *Dogmatics* where he speaks of "The Word of God and Faith." [6] And he repeats it over and over, in every possible manner. Faith is a re-cognition of the Word of God. Yet, whatever this means, it never implies that man of himself has the power to bring about this recognition.

> What [man] actually can and does compass is acknowledged by the acknowledged Word of God, not as self-determination, but as self-determination determined by the Word of God (p. 263).

> Granted that in faith and the profession of faith the Word of God becomes "human thought and human word,"

> by that is not meant an immanent transformation of human thought or human speech (pp. 276-277).

---

5. For a development of Barth's conception of faith, see H. Bouillard, *Karl Barth* (Paris, Aubier, 1957) vol. III, pp. 9-61.
6. *Church Dogmatics*, vol. 1, part 1; trans. by G. T. Thomson (Edinburgh, T. & T. Clark, 1960), pp. 260-283. In the pages that follow, parenthesized page numbers occurring in the text refer to this translation.

As Barth describes it, the occurrence of real faith should be thought of as the Word clearing a path for itself in man.

> We have to think of man in the event of real faith, as, so to speak, opened up from above (p. 278).
> This means that man, precisely as *believing* or *in the act of*

believing, rests not in himself but solely in the object of his act of believing, and furthermore, and again as *believing,* exists only in virtue of this object. Consequently, in believing or in the act of believing, man cannot conceive of himself as the subject who is performing the action or the work that is occurring in him.

> Man acts by believing [i.e. when he believes], but the fact that he believes by acting [when he acts] is God's act (p. 281).

In that case, does man have at least a "possibility," an "ableness" of his own to receive the Word? Barth spends a whole section explaining why the answer can only be negative.[7] It is true, he writes, that the Word of God must be understood as an event occurring in human reality and to this occurrence must correspond, logically and really, a human "possibility" or "capacity" (cf. pp. 220-221). Lest we think that Barth is actually giving an affirmative answer, we have to read on to see how this possibility is understood. That, after all, is the point of the question. The coming of the Word, does it in fact require a human possibility "that is brought to meet it, so to speak, by man as such," a kind of

> predisposition appertaining to him *qua* man from the start, in an organ, in a positive or even negative qualification to be reached and discovered by an anthropological analysis of existence; in short, in what philosophy of the Kantian type calls a "faculty" (p. 220)?

---

7. *Ibid.,* "The Knowability of the Word of God," pp. 213-283.

If the answer to this is no, then we must consider the alter-native, which is that the possibility resides in the event itself, in the coming of the Word, and through the event the possibility is established in man in such a way as to become possibility for man, and of man, but without ceasing to be "the Word of God's own potentiality, proper to it alone" (p. 221). If that is it, the human possibility of knowledge of the Word must be explained on the basis of its object or the reality known, and not on the basis of the knowing subject, man himself.

And this is how Barth understands it. It was for him the only acceptable explanation. It was also inevitable that it should be, for his doctrinal position regarding the Word of God compelled him. The Word of God, he says, is not truly a grace if man has, in and of himself, the possibility of knowing it (p. 221). The man who really knows the Word of God also knows quite clearly that he does not have within himself the capacity or faculty to know it (p. 224). Hence, the possibility of belief arises not from us but from the reality of the Word. As far as man the believer is concerned, the possibility, such as it is, is "given" to him or "lent" to him by God, and lent solely for use [not, presumably, for retention as properly his own] (p. 272). If, then, there is anything "common" between God who speaks and man who hears, a "point of contact" (so to speak), this occurs, if it occurs at all, in the presence and from the presence of the Word (p. 273). Consequently, it is futile to look for the aforesaid power or capa-city among those that are proper to man — and we had better all remind ourselves that

> the statement about the indwelling of Christ which takes place in faith may not be converted into an anthropological state-ment (p. 275).

Essentially, Barth is saying that man must indeed open the door to Christ (Apoc. 3:20), but if the door opens,

> even the fact of that event is, *quoad actum* and *quoad poten-*

tiam, the work of the Christ who stands outside. So that the other thing also remains unreservedly true, that the risen Christ passes through closed doors (Jn. 20: 19ff) [p. 283].

Clearly, then, in the Barthian view the act of "faith" is exclusively "from God." Recently again, in 1963 at a colloquy between Catholics and Protestants where the discussion centered on some cardinal theses of Christianity, Barth spoke to the same effect, that for Protestants *faith* means the human acceptance and acquisition of God's grace, but the acceptance and appropriation are already "under the dominion of grace." The Holy Spirit prepares man and moves him to sensory recognition of this grace (in the Word and sacrament) as well as to rational awareness, and furthermore, makes him experience it in his heart. Yet nowhere in the process — and this is decisive — can man say that "grace is at his disposal," to take or not to take, in the way he has at his disposal other things which he discovers, perceives and experiences. Even at the moment when God fills us with grace he dwells in light inaccessible, because man is a sinner, because community with God is not possible to man except through God's sole initiative, without any reciprocity from man, so that man can never "put his hand on God" as God puts his on man. At every instant and in every respect man is moved by God and by God alone — never by himself.[8]

In these circumstances, how does one really lay hold of the christian revelation, for it would seem to be beyond the reach and grasp of man, always hovering above or hastening by? And the act of faith, is it still man's act? Barth anticipates the challenge.[9] There is (he argues) a human experience of the Word of God. The experience moves man to make a choice, in which all his faculties are engaged. Man, that is, determines himself and the

---

8. *Catholiques et Protestants* (Paris, Éd. du Seuil, 1963). For the content of this paragraph see in particular pp. 162-163.
9. *Church Dogmatics,* "The Word of God and Experience," (English trans. pp. 226-260).

self-determination is real, psychologically speaking, but all it does is make way for the divine action. If that be the case, are we to assume that man as "believer" simply fades away, out of the picture, as God passes by? In other words, the experience of the Word, precisely as experience of the Word, is it still man's act or all God's doing, a passing through, as it were. These are pertinent questions, and they are echoed by the author of an acclaimed study of Barth who, while acknowledging the merits of his position and its skillful presentation, nevertheless feels bound to ask "whether man is truly the subject of the act by which he recognizes and acknowledges the divine revelation," or, in more graphic phrase, whether Barth "does not require the believer to outjump his shadow," and then whether faith in its most vital phase and reality is "more than a turn-around point in an excursion that finds God on a course away from himself and, at the given moment, returning again." In one simple question, has Barth remained faithful to the New Testament? [10]

The Church

Reconciliation comes about in the Church. "Outside the Church, no *revelation,* no *faith,* no *knowledge* of salvation," declares Barth.[11] The Church, as he conceives it, is the "living congregation of Jesus Christ, the living Lord." This is its *definition,* according to Barth. The Church,

the Congregation, *exists* to the extent that it receives the gift of deriving its own life from the work of its living Lord (p. 95).

---

10. *Op. cit.,* (cf. note 5), p. 17. We return to this point in Part Three of our study.
11. *Dogmatik* (Zurich, 1953) IV/1, p. 769. [English translation of this volume not yet available.] See also K. Barth, "L'Église, congrégation vivante de Jésus-Christ," in *Recueil des travaux de l'Assemblée du Conseil oecuménque des Églises à Amsterdam* (1948), vol. I, pp. 95-107. The citations which follow are taken from this article.

When the "current of life between the Lord and his congregation is broken," the realization (occurrence) of the congregation ceases to be a *realization*, the congregation ceases to be *alive*. In other words, "the Church passes from existence to non-existence" (p. 100). Instead of the Church,

> which is no longer the Church, there appears not nothing but the phenomenon of the pseudo-Church or the semblance of the Church, an ecclesiastical surrogate which has all the manifestations of the living congregation but without their inner substance (p. 100).

The Church, viz. the *local congregation,* is constituted by the possibility and the existence of regular, common divine service.

> The Church lives (it exists!) in virtue of this visible, concrete activity (profession of faith, baptism, Lord's Supper, proclamation and acceptance of the Good News); it lives in virtue of the prerequisite conditions (theology, catechetics) for such activity or divine service and in virtue of its consequences (fraternal discipline, care of souls and other forms of mutual assistance) (p. 103).

But — is this not "religion"? The question cannot be answered without taking into account the role of the ecclesiastical structure.

> The sense and purpose of every ecclesiastical structure is to unite the congregation in such a way that it will be as ready as possible for whatever the Lord, and he alone, can and wills to accomplish in it (p. 102).

The Lord alone acts — this is the point of it.

Not only is the local congregation united, but there are bonds of unity between local congregations as well. Barth describes them as "transversal connections," i.e., expressions and instruments of their unity in the form of freely-undertaken *community activities,* for the cause of charity, education, home and foreign missions (p. 105), but always "within the limits of the one gift and the one task by which the Church is the Church" (p. 105). Moreover, a "synodal congregation" could even

> guarantee as far as humanly possible, the coordination and solidarity of the local congregations that belong to it, establishing a spiritual rule with spiritual authority, as much attentive to necessary reforms as to maintaining the legitimate elements of tradition; ... a veritable mother congregation, [it] will give local congregations counsel and encouragement, issue directives and apply sanctions (pp. 104-105).

Yet for all that the synodal congregation may be called upon to do,

> the governing, properly speaking, of the Church must be and must remain the exclusive prerogative of the One Lord of all congregations (p. 105).

Significantly, the gatherings and meetings which Barth envisions are not called "religion," or the exercise of religion. In the article we have been citing he uses the term, but rather disparagingly. The Church, he remarks, is threatened when the congregation, forgetful of its specific task, burdens itself with "other preoccupations: the needs, the opinions and concerns individual to the 'Christians' gathered together" (p. 99). When that happens,

> faith in the gospel is replaced by the religiosity of Christians (p. 99).

And, moments later, he makes this observation:

> The Church herself has become a part of the world, a religious world; she is nothing more than a worldly prophetess, very proud and very superfluous (p. 100).

This, then, is the state of affairs that comes to his mind at the mention of the terms "religiosity" and "religious."

In the colloquy referred to earlier between Catholics and Protestants Barth spoke along the same lines.[12] In the Church, he asserted, we have to do with "a visible, historical greatness, discernible in men and human thought, in human institutions and achievements," the Church which in principle is "the place and the instrument of grace." But though "God's assistance comes to us in and through the Church, we do not on that account acquire any rights over him or over the things that are his only." We have indeed been given the Church and offered the divine assistance, yet "this does not mean that we have in our possession a right of some kind, or that this place and this instrument of grace, a visible, historical and human thing, has been entrusted to us as an instrument that would permit us to dispose of grace as we please and to *assure* ourselves of *guarantees* in regard to grace."

Karl Barth's opposition to 19th century Protestantism is not without greatness of its own. We are impressed when, in the felicitous manner of the master, he develops and re-develops the fundamental truth that there can be no bond, no kinship between God and man except on God's terms and God's initiative. We also nod approval when he reminds us that religion must not seek its strength in itself, as though it was the Source of salvation. But does he not exceed his purpose and even the demands of truth when he defines religion as he does, in such a simplistic manner? We shall return to this point in the middle section, where we inquire into the content of the christian revelation and the teaching of Christ. In the Barthian sense, religion — even the christian religion — is evil, radically evil. Today, no doubt, he would be more considerate of man's role and activity. Yet all in

---

12. See *Catholiques et Protestants,* pp. 163-164.

all, Barth's conception of religion is, to say no more, incomplete. At the same time it would be most unfair to single out his exaggerations or impetuous utterances as pretext for pell-mell rejection of sacraments, creeds and ecclesiastical structures. Those who are declaiming that "the christian revelation is the abolition of religion" should re-read his Amsterdam discourse, "The Church, Living Congregation of Jesus Christ the Living Lord." [13]

---

13. An over-all introduction to Barth available in English is Jerome Hamer, O.P., *Karl Barth;* trans. by Dominic M. Maruca (Westminster, Md., Newman Press, 1962) — [Tr.]

II

The Emptiness of Religions

A much-mentioned name nowadays is Dietrich Bonhoeffer, German pastor and theologian. Born in Breslau in 1906, he fell into the hands of the Gestapo and was put to death by hanging April 9, 1945.[1]

A collection of letters and other pieces he wrote during his two-year imprisonment in Berlin was subsequently published under the title *Widerstand und Ergebung* (Resistance and Submission). With one or two exceptions, our citations will be confined to this work, in which we find this estimate of Barth:

> He brought in against religion the God of Jesus Christ, *"pneuma against sarx."* That remains his greatest service . . . . It was not in ethics, as is often said, that he subsequently failed . . . ; it was that in the nonreligious interpretation of theological concepts he gave no concrete guidance, either in dogmatics or in ethics (pp. 180-181).[2]

1. An outstanding French work on the life and thought of Bonhoeffer is R. Marlé, *Dietrich Bonhoeffer, témoin de Jésus-Christ parmi ses frères* (Tournai-Paris, Casterman, 1967). Many English works are also available, among others W. Kuhns, *In Pursuit of Dietrich Bonhoeffer*. With a Foreword by Eberhard Bethge (London, Burns and Oates, 1967). [This is a good general introduction — Tr.]
2. *Letters and Papers from Prison*, pp. 180-181; trans. of *Widerstand und Ergebung* by Reginald Fuller and revised by Frank Clarke and others (London, S. C. M. Press, 1967). American edition published as *Prisoner for God* (3rd edition, with revised translation; New York, The Macmillan Co., 1967. Paperback, *Letters and Papers from Prison*, 1962). [English citations are from S. C. M. edition.]

"Nonreligious interpretation of theological concepts." It is not difficult to see why expressions and passages like this should make Bonhoeffer a favorite among those who are engaged in the contemporary depreciation of religions and indeed of religion as such. But the reality of the present situation is far more complex. And so is Bonhoeffer's thought.

The Pastoral Problem

The letters, notes and documents assembled in *Widerstand und Ergbung* [title of the English translation is *Letters and Papers from Prison*] cover the period of April 5, 1943 to January 17, 1945 and are arranged in chronological order. In them are reflected the spiritual and theological ferment that stirred in Bonhoeffer's soul during the prison years. This inner search and struggle helps us to understand and evaluate some of his more provocative ideas. Expressed paradoxically, they compel attention — we find ourselves stopping to think them over.

Bonhoeffer begins with reality, with the world as it is, and his concern is unequivocally pastoral. We are moving, he says, in the direction of a completely religionless era. People as they are today simply cannot be religious any more. On the other hand, christian revelation and christian doctrine, grown old after 1900 years and more, rest on the supposition, the *a priori* of a religious mankind. Christianity, by the way, has always been a religion, perhaps the true one. But if one day it is discovered that the *a priori* no longer exists but was a form of human expression, historically conditioned and perishable, and that instead men have become "radically religionless," — what does that bode for Christianity?

What do a church, a community, a sermon, a liturgy, a christian life mean in a religionless world? How do we speak

---

To avoid unnecessary multiplication of footnotes, citations from this work are identified in the text itself in the parenthesized page numbers.

of God — without religion, i.e., without the temporally conditioned presuppositions of metaphysics, inwardness [spirit-
uality?], and so on. How do we speak (or perhaps we cannot
now even "speak" as we used to) in a "secular" way about
"God"? In what way are we "religionless-secular" Christians
... (p. 153)?

How did this situation come about? In general, it developed
from the fact that man has learned to cope with all questions
of importance without recourse to the "hypothesis" called "God."
In questions of science and art, and even in "ethics," this is to
be expected. But for the last hundred years or so it has also
become true of "religious questions," so that apparently "everything gets along without 'God' — and, in fact, just as well as
before" (p. 178). In the scientific field God has been losing
ground for a long time, but today he is being pushed out of every
sector of human affairs. He is, in short, "losing more and more
ground" everywhere (p. 178).

God is being increasingly pushed out of a world that has
come of age, out of the spheres of our knowledge and life,
and ... since Kant he has been relegated to a realm beyond
the world of experience (p. 188).

God, argues Bonhoeffer, has been "used" as a "stop-gap,"
the answer to questions we could not solve (p. 174), a *deus
ex machina* to whom we resort when "human knowledge has
met its limits." Since these limits are constantly expanding, God
has become, or will one day become, altogether "superfluous"
(p. 154).

But this is not the true God, the God of the Bible? There
is a crucial difference between the God of the Bible and the God
of religions, and it is this:

Man's religiosity makes him look in his distress to the power
of God in the world: God is the *deus ex machina*. The Bible

directs man to God's powerlessness and suffering; only the suffering God can help. To that extent we may say that the development towards the world's coming of age outlined above, which has done away with a false conception of God, opens up a way of seeing the God of the Bible, who wins power and space in the world by his weakness (p. 197).[3]

According to Bonhoeffer it is here, in the God of weakness, where the "secular interpretation" must begin (p. 197).

But if there is a God of the Bible, and a Jesus Christ, it would seem that there is also a religion. But not so. In the New Testament, he explains, we find that man is "caught up into the messianic suffering of God in Jesus Christ" in a variety of ways (p. 199). Jesus calls the disciples, heals the sick, receives the shepherds, the Magi and the little ones, without regard to their moral conversion, their poverty and needs.

The only thing that is common to all these is their sharing in the suffering of God in Christ. That is their "faith." There is nothing of religious method here. The "religious act" is always something partial; "faith" is something whole, involving the whole of one's life. Jesus calls men, not to a new religion, but to life (p. 199).

Repudiation of "Religion"

One naturally wonders why Bonhoeffer should harbor such mistrust, indeed such opposition toward all religion, why "religion" should arouse in him this hostile reaction. Sometimes, it appears, it is for the same reasons we found in Barth.

The Pauline question whether περιτομή [i.e., circumcision] is a condition of justification seems to me in present-day terms

---

3. This theme predominates in W. H. Hamilton's *The New Essence of Christianity* (New York, 1961). Hamilton is one of the foremost spokesmen of the "death of God" theology.

to be whether religion is a condition of salvation. Freedom from περιτομή is also freedom from religion (p. 154).

Another clue to his attitude toward religion is his criticism of apologetics. He does not think apologetics is "christian" when it

confuses Christ with one particular stage in man's religiousness, i.e., with a human law (p. 179).

While Bonhoeffer does not press the point, nevertheless in comparing religion to circumcision and therefore to the Old Testament dispensation he makes it quite clear what his sentiments are. Like circumcision, religion is a thing of the past, or at least old and decrepit — on its way out. But there is still more.

Many times when Bonhoeffer declares himself against a "religious" Christianity, he has in mind a specific view of religion, a pietistic conception. This is important to remember. And it may suggest that a first reading of a passage is not always enough. For example, we cannot but be struck, the first time we read *Letters and Papers From Prison,* by something he says in a letter dated November 21, 1943.

I have found that following Luther's instruction to 'make the sign of the cross' at our morning and evening prayers is in itself helpful. There is something objective about it, and that is what is particularly badly needed here. Don't be alarmed; I shall not come out of here a *homo religiosus.*[4] My distrust and my dread of religion are greater than ever (p. 97).

When we learn that a Lutheran pastor makes the sign of the cross yet does not want to be a religious man, *homo religiosus,* we are indeed left wondering — wondering what he could possibly mean by "religious" and "religiousness." Quite probably, as we have suggested, he is referring to the sort of pietism he found so distasteful and lashed out against on many occasions.

---

4. Italicized in the original.

Heim sought, along pietist and Methodist lines, to convince the individual man that he was faced with the alternative "despair or Jesus." He gained "hearts" (p. 180).

In Bonhoeffer's view this way of stating it, despair or Jesus, is a fraud, utterly contrary to his way of thinking. He takes sharp issue with those who, in the pattern of "christian apologetics" (pp. 178-179), try to convince man that he is miserable and unhappy in order to win him over to God as the only answer to this "ultimate question" of existence. Existentialist philosophy and psychotherapy, he charges, are guilty of this in their own way. For the existentialists and psychotherapists try to prove to man that even though he is or thinks himself confident and happy and content, he is actually unhappy and in despair but unwilling to admit it, that he is in the grip of deep distress without knowing it and from which only they can rescue him. It is in this regard that Bonhoeffer labels them as "secularized offshoots of christian theology" and their method as "secularized Methodism" (p. 179). In short, a God who is God only as the antidote to man's unhappiness is not the true God. It is this sort of manipulation, he adds, that I rise up against (p. 189).

To Bonhoeffer Methodist pietism was thoroughly repugnant. We have seen the reason — because God is thought of and urged upon man as the solution to a no-relief situation, where man throws up his hands in utter failure: i.e., man in his misery and despair. Yet this pietism is only a case in point. In Bonhoeffer's view all religion was without foundation and substance, a superfluous thing, because every religion strives to demonstrate God to the world by offering him as the solution to situations that exceed man's resources and capabilities, and this in every department of human life: science, art, ethics, religion, and the rest. In other words, every religion "exploits" the limits of man, and when these limits are exhausted, introduces a "stop-gap" God, a *deus ex machina*:

Religious people speak of God when human knowledge . . .

has come to an end, or when human resources fail — in fact it is always the *deus ex machina* that they bring on to to the scene, either for the apparent solution of insoluble problems, or as strength in human failure — always, that is to say, exploiting human weakness or human boundaries. Of necessity, that can go on only till people can by their own strength push these boundaries somewhat further out, so that God becomes superfluous as a *deus ex machina* (p. 154).

Confronted with limits it is better, he contends, to be silent and not try to solve the unsolvable. We should speak of God not on the boundaries but at the center. God is in the midst of our life without ceasing to be "beyond." And the Church appears not where human powers fail, not at the boundaries but "in the middle of the village" (p. 155).

Consequently a "religionless Christianity" is a Christianity that is rid of an "historically conditioned and transient form of human self-expression" (p. 152), rid of a "garment" which even as a garment has looked very different at different times (p. 153). What is required is not that Christ be "the object of religion" but something far different, "Lord of the world" (pp. 153-154), "Lord of the religionless" (p. 153).

At this point, in keeping with his pastoral concern, Bonhoeffer again raises the question of preaching. How are we to interpret and proclaim a religionless Christianity? How to

re-interpret in a "worldly" sense — in the sense of the Old Testament and of John 1:14 — the concepts of repentance, faith, justification, rebirth, and sanctification (p. 157)?

And, in the same vein, how do we speak in a "secular" way about God? And how are we to be "religionless-secular" Christians? It is impossible, he believes, to know just how this metamorphosis will come about. For the time being, however, this can be said:

Our earlier words [forms of preaching] are bound to lose

their force and cease, our being Christians today will be limited
to two things: prayer and righteous action among men. All
christian thinking, speaking, and organizing must be born
anew out of this prayer and action. By the time you have
grown up,[5] the Church's form will have changed greatly (p.
172).

Christian Existence

We have just seen how Bonhoeffer poses the "pastoral problem." However, to appreciate the true dimensions of this German
thinker we must not limit ourselves to this particular problem
but consider his life as a whole. From 1935 to 1937 he was rector
of a theological seminary at Finkenwalde. There, he and his
students entered upon an authentic conventual life, which he
had to defend against detractors. It was a regime that engaged
in genuine spiritual formation. It included common prayer, study,
fraternal correction and, in time, even confession as well as
celebration of the Lord's Supper — a "community life" of peace
and quiet along the cliffs of Finkenwalde.[6] The spiritual experience
of these years [7] is recounted in a circular letter to his "brethren."
On March 1, 1942 he recalls what the daily meditation means
to him, and should mean to them:

Quiet, daily meditation on the Word of God as it relates to my
life, even if no more than a few minutes duration, must be for
me the point round which turns everything that makes for ex-
terior and interior order in my life. In these times when the

---

5. The reference is to Bonhoeffer's godson, born in February, 1944. This
   passage occurs in the "Reflections" he wrote in May of the same year,
   on the occasion of the child's baptism.
6. See R. Marlé, *op. cit.*, (cf. note 1), p. 25.
7. Translations respectively of *Gemeinsames Leben* and *Nachfolge*, of the
   first by J. W. Doberstein (New York, Harper and Brothers, 1954), of
   the second by R. H. Fuller (Revised and unabridged edition, containing
   material not previously translated; New York, The Macmillian Co., 1959.
   Paperback edition, 1963).

customary regulation of our life is necessarily disrupted and when the danger is great that even inner peace and order will be jeopardized by the rapid succession of events and the monopolizing demands of work and service, in these times, I say, meditation introduces a kind of stability into our life. It maintains a continuity with our past life, from baptism to confirmation and ordination. It keeps us in salutary communion with our spiritual brethren and our spiritual fireside. It is a spark of the fireside which the communities wish to provide for you here. It is a source of peace and patience and joy, a magnet which polarizes and orientates all the means we have for bringing order into our life. It is like the smooth surface of deep water in which the sky, both with its clouds and its bright sun, appears in vivid reflection.[8]

On November 18, 1943 he wrote the following to a friend:

I also felt it to be an omission not to have carried out my long-cherished wish to attend the Lord's Supper once again with you . . . and yet I know that we have shared spiritually, although not physically, in the gift of confession, absolution, and communion . . . . At the moment I am trying to write some prayers for prisoners; it is surprising that there are none, and perhaps these may be distributed at Christmas . . . . Let us promise to remain faithful in interceding for each other. I shall ask that you may have strength, health, patience, and protection from conflicts and temptations. You can ask for the same things for me (pp. 88-89).

Doubtless, an author's thought can change and grow, but rarely does he renounce all that he has preached and practiced for years and years. And though Bonhoeffer wrestled with the question of a "religionless Christianity" throughout most

8. [My translation of this passage is from the French text which the author quotes from Marlé, *op. cit.,* p. 27 — Tr.]

of his career, it was during his last year on earth that the struggle became most acute. It is interesting to note, therefore, that in May, 1944, when he learned that his nephew was going to be baptized, he wrote to him about baptism and the Church of the future. Your parents, he says in effect, will teach you "to say your prayers, to fear and love God above everything, and to do the will of Jesus Christ" (p. 165). This reference to prayer occurs constantly in his letters. On May 20, 1944 he wrote:

> There is always the danger that intense love may cause one to lose what I might call the polyphony of life. What I mean is that God wants us to love him with our whole hearts — not in such a way as to injure or weaken our earthly love, but to provide a kind of *cantus firmus* to which the other melodies of life provide the counterpoint. One of their contra- puntal themes (which have their own complete independence but are yet related to the *cantus firmus*) is earthly affection . . . . Where the *cantus firmus* is clear and plain, the counterpoint can be developed to its limits. The two are "undivided and yet distinct," in the words of the Chalcedonian Definition, like Christ in his divine and human natures (p. 162).

In the aforementioned letter to his nephew he adverts to what he believes to be the hollowness and ineffectiveness of contemporary preaching. But a new era (he feels) is coming. Meanwhile, "our being Christians . . . will be limited to two things: prayer and righteous action among men" (p. 172). And, pending the day that men will again be called to proclaim the Word of God,

> the christian cause will be a silent and hidden affair, but there will be those who pray and do right and wait for God's own time. May you be one of them . . . (p. 172).

Bonhoeffer, "religionless" and "secular," never forgets prayer, nor sacraments. "Religionless Christians" could take a cue from that.

III

A "Secular" Religion

When the leaders of the National Student Christian Federation of the United States asked Harvey Cox, university professor
and Baptist minister, to conduct a series of conferences on Christianity, they never suspected that within a few months the conferences that were to become *The Secular City* would be a world-
wide success.[1] Nor, for that matter, did the author. In the Preface
to the Revised Edition he notes that his purpose was quite limited
and specific: to persuade his audience of young, intelligent and
mainly Protestant lay people that "in the light of Biblical faith,
secularization and urbanization do not represent sinister curses
to be escaped, but epochal opportunities to be embraced." Within
a year the book went through more than ten printings in the
United States.

In *The Secular City* the christian church is again subjected
to some criticism, which the author believes is warranted by the
gospel itself. Doubtless, many of Cox's judgments are too hastily
formed, and exegetes will not always be happy with his way of
interpreting the Bible. Even so, the book is growing in popularity
in Europe, and while it may not be destined to become the
phenomenal success that it has been in the United States, it
can nevertheless boast of a number of punchlines that may be
depended on to strike the popular fancy because of the truth

---

1. Harvey Cox, *The Secular City,* (Subtitle: Secularization and Urbanization in Theological Perspective.) Revised Edition. New York, The
   Macmillan Co., 1966.
   As in the previous chapters, citations and references are identified in
   the text proper through parenthesized page numbers.

they contain. But what attracts the popular attention may not be the substantive message. And that is what we propose to deal with, viz., some of the more basic premises developed in the book, and we trust that the discussion will serve to keep the author from having intentions attributed to him which he does not have and does not want to have.

According to Cox, the two outstanding features of contemporary civilization are general urbanization and the collapse of traditional religion. Ours is the age of the "city of man." It is the product of social evolution, in which three stages are discernible: the tribe, the town and the gigantic city, which he names "technopolis." The social organization of each stage conditions and determines the form of religion — or nonreligion — that it will have. Mankind is moving toward the technopolis. The movement is inevitable. There is no stopping it. But what kind of religion will it bring? A "secularized religion"? Or no religion at all? We shall attend to this question somewhat later. To be noted, before that, are the characteristics of the city of man, the technopolis — in Cox's phrase, "the wave of the future."

One of its characteristics is *anonymity*. Modern man has become a "faceless cipher." Anonymity, then, can lead to depersonalization. But it also permits of freer and more selective choice of friends, leisures, social activities. It can, in short, safeguard what is genuinely human. At the same time it also calls for those broader relationships that are secondary rather than primary, functional rather than organic — how we meet the repairman, the bank clerk, the milkman, etc. These relationships also have their value and validity. The Samaritan helped the wounded man very effectively, without becoming his personal friend. Modern society needs both relationships, the private and the public, but in proper balance.

Modern society is also characterized by *mobility*. This may raise some doubt, for we are perhaps more inclined to think of the typical man of today as seated immobile before his desk, poring over records and documents and what not. And so he is. But is he not also, and more so, a man on the go, a man behind

the steering wheel of an impatient automobile? Social analysts
have studied geographic and occupational mobility. Not enough
attention, however, has been paid to mobility as a condition of
human and social progress.

Finally, the technopolis has its *culture*, which is dominated
by "pragmatism" and "profanity." Cox recognizes that he is using
these terms at the risk of some confusion, but he is taking them
in their original or even literal sense, pragmatism referring to
man's concern with the question "will it work?" and profanity
to man's wholly secular horizon and his dismissal of other-worldly
reality as a factor in life. For technopolitan man life "is a set
of problems, not an unfathomable mystery." This world, not
some kind of world above, is his proper domain. Should theologians try to "de-secularize" him? Not at all, says Cox. Secular
man is not necessarily sacrilegious. He is unreligious, and his
very unreligiosity enables him "to discern certain elements of
the gospel which were hidden from his more religious forebears"
(p. 54).

According to Cox, the discernment of rehabilitation of the
true biblical concept of God is a case in point. Traditional christian theism, he contends, has had a defective notion of God,
an intermixture of the God of the Bible with Plato's Idea of the
Good or Aristotle's Prime Mover. It was this marred image of
God that led Camus, for example, to believe that one had to
choose *between* God and human freedom, between christian faith
and human creativity (p. 67). Camus chose freedom and rejected
God but it was the God of traditional christian theism he rejected
and, says Cox, "rightly, I believe." Yet it must not be thought that
the "difference between men of faith and serious skeptics is
merely verbal. There are genuine differences between the two
which cannot be overlooked. But it is precisely to uncover and
clarify these real differences that we must expose and discard
the unreal ones" (p. 67).

The Church in the Secular City

What is the mission of the Church in the age of the *technopolis?* A Baptist, Cox quite naturally thinks of the Church as a christian community, though he has little enthusiasm for its institutional aspects. Too often, he feels, we deal with problems of the Church as institutional problems. Yet the Church is not the institutions but the "people of God," whose institutions have no other purpose than to set God's people on their course and promote their participation in God's action in the world, which consists in "the liberation of man to freedom and responsibility" (p. 108).

God's action works through social change, but we need to know where this action in which we are to participate is located. Hence, we need a theology of what theologians have called "historical events" but which Cox prefers to name "social change," and we need it before a theology of the Church itself. We can then locate the action — the location is in the life of Jesus of Nazareth. The Church's ministry is to continue the threefold ministry of Jesus, comprising *kerygma* (proclamation), *diakonia* (reconciliation, healing, service in general) and *koinonia* (demonstration of the character of the new society) [p. 110]. In addition, the Church today must also exercise the important function of "exorcist." In performing its multiple task the Church becomes the "avant-garde of God" (p. 125) and the "avant-garde of the new regime" (p. 110).

Kerygma, or message, proclaims that God has overcome the "principalities and powers" through Jesus. He has made us "heirs," i.e., masters of the created world. The world, then, has been "defatalized," i.e., rescued from fate's dominion over it. Control now lies with man. It is for him to direct the powers, to utilize them in freedom and responsibility as, in the biblical term, a "son," — son of God exercising freedom and responsibility before God in his rule over the powers, the forces in a culture which cripple and corrupt human freedom" (p. 110). As avant-garde, the Church is to proclaim the "new era" which is already begun. The christian attitude toward the world is positive, dynamic;

the christian message urges to social change. As a result of this message history is in permanent "crisis," the old regime in never-ending conflict with the new. Easter and Exodus are the two facts that dominate the whole theology of the Church: Exodus because it shows that God really wills the liberation of man, Easter because it shows that his liberating activity is still at work today.

Diakonia has reference to "service," as some translate it. But "service" (Cox believes) has been so cheapened "that it retains little significance." What it really expresses is the "act of healing and reconciling" (p. 114), bringing together the conflicting groups of urban society: center-city vs. suburbs, haves vs. have nots, whites vs. blacks and, more generally, ethnic and racial divisions, political parties. In short, *diakonia* works toward the restoration of the health and wholeness of the secular city.

Koinonia, usually translated "fellowship," provides the secular city with a living demonstration of the Church's kerygma and diakonia, with the first fruits, as it were, of the "character and composition of the true city of man for which the Church strives" (p. 125). The Church, then, is the "eschatological community," those who already live by the ethos of the new era, in the style of the new regime, the product of God's activity. The Church, in its *koinoniac* aspect, is the advance realization, the forerunner of God's design for all mankind. Most prominent in the *koinoniac* function is the overcoming of religious and cultic divisions: Jews and Gentiles, clean and unclean (pp. 125, 126).

This outline of the Church's mission is more or less the theory of it. How is it to be realized in practice? Cox illustrates it from three major aspects of the social order, chosen (no doubt) with an eye to the public to which he was addressing his book. The aspects are: work, sex, the university. However, before discussing them Cox introduces a chapter on the Church as Cultural Exorcist, because "exorcism remains the point at which the three aspects of the Church's ministry come closest to fusing" (p. 130). Thus, the multiple ministries of the Church are brought together under a more general rule of action for the People of God, the community of Christians, namely in the Church's activity as exorcist.

Jesus, Cox observes, cast out "demons." Moreover, his exorcisms were "in no way peripheral, but stood at the heart of his work" (p. 130). Even in the age of the secular city, in the new regime, there are many demons to cast out. Cox illustrates what he means by citing the psychoanalytic theory of repression and projection. When we have feelings, e.g., of hostility or sexuality, which society prohibits us from expressing, we either redirect them into some other form of activity (sublimation) or transfer them onto other persons or things — Jews and Negroes are mentioned. This is a modern version of exorcism, or rather one phase of it, for the "casting out of demons necessitates dealing both with those who have projected the spurious identities and with those who have introjected them." In the case of the Negro it includes, as Martin Luther King remarked, "*both* changing the prejudice of the white man *and* overcoming the 'slave mentality' in the Negro" (p. 132).

Jesus dealt with neuroses of the individual. But the Church has also to be concerned with collective neuroses, with exorcisms of the cultural and social order. In either case, in collective as in individual neurosis, the aim of exorcism is to free the exorcised from, in Freudian phrase, an "archaic heritage," which limits the freedom of the neurotic and creates "a phantom world through repression and projection" (p. 133). Cox cites the attitude of American society toward the Negro as one of the collective neuroses that need to be exorcised.

All in all, the tasks of the Church of the technopolitan age are not basically different from what they were before. Nevertheless, the social conditions are far different, and the differences call for a restructuring of the Church and its pastoral organization. The residential parish, in particular, is no longer adequate, though still having a function. In general, it will be necessary to improve upon or supersede all those institutional forms which predate the industrial era, before the rise of urbanization. Our faith in God should tell us that he can renew and revitalize his Church to meet the exigencies of the secular city. They key word in the task of re-vitalization is *differentiation*. In a society that is becoming differen-tiated at a faster pace than ever before, the Church also must demonstrate an ever-widening differentiation of structure, increasing specialization of Church life and activity. Moreover, restructuring and renewal are never finished. In a rapidly changing society like ours they can never stand still but must be constantly in progress.

Accordingly, the work of exorcising myths and demons is perennial. And exorcised they must be because they distort man's vision of reality and constrict his behavior. As noted earlier, some of these "demons" are examined in detail, namely those affecting work, sex, and the university. Urbanization and secularization, Cox observes, has had an enormous impact on work, bringing new problems but also opportunities never found before.

For example, in the technopolitan society the place of work tends to be away from the place of residence. Specialization of work demands the concentration of workers. The result is that work and family life are kept apart. Work, in other words, is "de-familiarized." Most people, in Cox's view, want it that way. Industrial concentration bars the paternalism that seems to be a trait of small businesses. Cox views the demise of the small business or the small farm with approval. The technopolitan age is the age of the organization, which is here to stay. It has advantages. It is flexible, future-oriented, secularized and makes only a "limited claim on its members." By contrast, the "orders" or integrative principles of the past (guild, tribe, clan, polis) encompassed most, if not all, of the aspects of social existence. They were traditional and conservative, and encumbered by ethnic or religious con-siderations. Christians should revise their preaching and take into account this phenomenon of our time, this new way of society, the organization. They should try to direct it toward the good of others, the common good. Today it isn't just a question of "saving my soul." Man must be concerned for his neighbor, and show it by getting into the fray for control of the organization and by the responsible use of power.

Not only is work removed from residence. Work is also emancipated — Cox's term — from religion. The technopolitan society makes it possible for the first time in history to produce enough goods for everyone. Such obstacles as exist are not primarily political but religious. The obstacles can be traced to misunderstanding of the doctrine of vocation, the notion that God calls people to their particular job or profession. Work, in consequence, is shrouded in "religious mystery" and invested with "sacral significance." The job becomes inviolate — you may not leave it. The secular city, on the other hand, demands a "secularized" definition and concept of work, built around the principle of *cybernation,* the hitching of automation to cybernetics, of the machine to the computer. Thanks to cybernation, all people can have a share in the goods of this world. And whereas the Calvinist doctrine of predestination had the effect, in the Western Protestant world, of substituting work for religious devotion — work, in fact, became a religion — cybernation tends in the opposite direction, the secularization of work. Technopolitan man will see the positive values of cybernation, especially the enormously increased productivity it makes possible. Let us, then, have done with "vocation" to work and recognize instead its secular character. For the secularization of work is upon us, and society either adjusts to it or risks extinction.

But however much work may still be in the grip of "neurotic compulsiveness and religious mystery," this is far more the case in the area of sex, for "no aspect of human life seethes with so many unexorcised demons as does sex" (p. 167). Nowhere else are so many "mythical and metalogical" factors at work. The Miss America pageant, for example, is a residual cult of the pagan fertility goddesses. Miss America herself symbolizes the ideal young woman, the Girl. Her power is sex. "Sexuality is the basic form of all human relationship, and therein lies its terror and its power" (p. 177).

This power is being exploited, commercially. Indeed, "commercial exploitation of sex drives — not the call girl — is our most serious form of prostitution today" (p. 186). A glaring example is the magazine *Playboy*. Yet this magazine, as well as its "less successful imitators," is not really a "sex magazine" at all. It is basically antisexual, diluting and dissipating authentic sexuality. Cox makes a detailed analysis of the social import of *Playboy,* capping it with a searching theological criticism. Primarily, the Miss America mystique and the *Playboy* philosophy are immoral because they pander to man's egocentricity. Sex is pursued for what it is for me, not for others. It becomes a pastime. Others, especially women, become the Playboy's playthings. The Playboy and Miss America are idols of American civilization. "Anything that functions, even in part, as a god when it is in fact not God, is an idol" (p. 171). Idols are destructive and despotic. Whoever lives by them becomes their captive, prevented by them from achieving human maturity and a proper sense of responsibility. Sorely needed is a liberating action, the exorcism of these "demons."

Furthermore, while on the one hand young people are constantly bombarded with erotic stimuli of one kind or another — e.g., through advertising, fashion designs, entertainment media — there still lingers the ethic of the Puritan and Victorian past, at least "on paper." This contradiction creates tension and confusion among unmarried young adults. At this point Cox introduces a lengthy discussion of the traditional stand concerning premarital relations, not necessarily to justify them but to expose the hypocrisy of a society that is sex-saturated on the one hand yet turns thumbs down on premarital sex. What should Christians do about all this? Cox has some advice. In general, in the area of sex as in others, Christians should promote a Gospel ethic, not a Law ethic. A Gospel ethic "demands more maturity and more discipline than a Law ethic." And even though it is "riskier," the risk must be taken because it is the "Gospel and not the Law that saves" (p. 184).

As regards universities, the Church has never quite reconciled itself to the fact that its hold on them is "either gone or fast disappearing." Like other institutions of our culture, the university is in the process of secularization, if not already secularized. At some points, as a matter of fact, the university itself takes the lead in this process. Yet even though the university has become a secularized institution, the Church for the most part cannot be said to have adapted itself successfully to this social change. The institutional Church still remains wedded to the organization and theology it had in the late 19th century. One of the attempts it made to meet the university problem in America was to establish its own colleges and universities. But this is "medievalism." Sometimes the Church seems to act as though its pastoral mission was fulfilled by building churches, on or off campuses. The harsh truth is that the Church has not yet found a way to relate in any effective manner to the university and the student community. Happily, however, there are appearing on the university scene certain student movements created by students themselves with a genuine interest in promoting ecumenical (as against denominational) life on the campus. Such groups, Cox believes, are signs of hope.

In all this concern over the Church's position vis-a-vis the university we need to keep in mind that the Church is more than buildings and organizations. It is an "event," a "happening." It is a proclamation of the day when there will be "no more Jew nor Greek, slave nor free," a demonstration of divisions healed and rivalries ceased. It cannot be simply identified with the organizations that have preempted the name to themselves. God's work of salvation can assert itself within the institutional Church, but also without. Faith must discern where the Church of Christ is stirring, where the work of the Lord is going on. Summing it up, Cox would say that the task of the Church in the university, the task of the "people of God in motion," would be as follows:

1. *Reconciliation*: The Church is always the instrument of reconciliation. This, in fact, is the primary calling of the people of God, the *laos theou*. As regards the university, it means reconciling rival groups of whatever kind: between departments, between the sciences and the humanities, teachers and administrators, town and gown, between racial, ethnic or creedal groups. Whatever the ideological or theological or religious differences may be, it is

a privilege to be ambassador for reconciliation, the privilege of the *laos theou.*

2. *Creative Criticism*: Christians in the university should be intellectually qualified, but they should also exercise their prophetic function, which they do through creative criticism. This is a task of the Church that has particular relevance in the university. As intellectuals, it is the business of Christians in the university to "think otherwise," not because of a perverse nature but as a necessary feature of society. The university itself must be challenged "to be the university." Criticism is the challenge. Furthermore, ideological pluralism is a "hallmark" of our time, an aspect of "secularization." Christians should face up to it and, instead of arguing over ideological differences, center their criticism on controllable, manageable issues that affect the lives of all of us. Moreover, Christians who live in the university community are, in a way, lay theologians. Like professional theologians, they have a responsibility to criticize Church life and organization, but clearly and intelligently. It is imperative that they meet this responsibility, for the Church is the Church "only when it is *semper reformanda,* when it is constantly being corrected and called back to its real task by the Word of God" (p. 201).

[Cox mentions yet a third point: *creative disaffiliation.* This, as the term implies, refers to the necessity of working "outside" the Church when its responsibilities to the world are not met from "inside" — Translator's note.]

God in the Secular City

Cox concludes his study with a chapter on God titled (in echo of Bonhoeffer) "To Speak in a Secular Fashion of God." While the problem of God has sociological and political implications, it is essentially a theological question. The God of the Christian faith is by nature *absconditus,* hidden. True, he reveals himself, but in ways and places he chooses, not as we might wish. He is unconditionally *for* man yet different *from* man and absolutely beyond "using" *by* man. His utter hiddenness is what distinguishes

God from tribal deities and the metaphysical deities with which philosophers round out their ontological systems.

Jesus, a theophany, an "appearance of God" beyond compare, does not change this. In Jesus, God does not cease to be hidden. He is not seen in himself or his essence. He continues to be utterly different from what men have wanted or expected of their God. In Jesus, God still meets man as the unavailable "other," but he does show man that he acts, even in his hiddenness, in human history. He teaches man, as Bonhoeffer says, to become mature and to get along without him by assuming his responsibility as an adult human. But responsibility means to be responsible *for* something *before* someone. Man must answer to God for his acts. And this is what makes the difference between theists and nontheists, something more than word play. The difference is over a reality. Indeed, between the "God who absents himself" and the "no-god-at-all" there is all the difference in the world, as there is between faith and nonfaith. However, the

difference between men of biblical faith and serious nontheists is not that we do not encounter the same reality. The difference is that we give that reality a different *name,* and in naming it differently, we differ seriously in the way we respond (pp. 227-228).

Furthermore, even though secular man may experience the transcendent in a radically different *way* from his forebears, the fact is he still encounters it. He may find it "in the nearest Thou at hand" (Bonhoeffer). But wherever he finds it, it must be "in and through the secular," i.e., in "the world and not overhead" (Amos Wilder). In short, the transcendent is still present — present in this "one-story world" of secular man.

Cox puts much stress on the "name" we give God, for in naming him we reflect the social structure of society. Symbols for God are drawn from some aspect of social life. "Father" suggests family relationships. "King" echoes political life or town culture. "Shep-

herd" is an occupational designation. When the social structure
changes, the symbols change, not without disturbance to faith.
Authority patterns also vary with culture and determine how man
conceives of his relationship with God. In tribal cultures authority
patterns are horizontal, in town cultures vertical. In technopolitan
culture both of these are being replaced by a "work team" pattern.
Theologically stated, in tribal society man participates in God,
who is never experienced as fully "other." In town culture, marked
as it is by vertical authority, the relationship between God and
man tends to be of the "I-Thou" type, one of confrontation, God
being regarded as *over* me. In the technopolitan culture of urban
society a new relationship seems to be emerging, comparable, as
we have said, to the "work team" pattern. Rather than participation
or confrontation, it is a relationship of *alongsidedness* — call it an
"I-You" partnership.

Cox suggests that these notions of work team and partnership
should receive more attention in our conceptualization of God.
In Jesus of Nazareth God showed that "he is willing to put himself
in the position of working within a group, of washing his fellows'
feet and of needing someone to carry his cross" (p. 231). In fact,
God does not even balk at being a "junior partner." Modern
man, for that matter, is less interested in knowing the nature of
God than in working together with him doing a common task. Of
course, this kind of relationship will not satisfy the individual who
has a compulsion to "experience" God. There will always be such
people, "religious questers," seeking spiritual experiences, but their
kind of questing runs counter to the "grain of the Bible." Admittedly, the Bible gives instances of mystic search and finding, but
throughout the Bible God makes it clear he is more interested in
seeing justice done and neighbor served.

How, then, are we to name this God who inclines more to
our "acts of mercy" than to our "fasting and cultic adoration"?
Will it still be "God"? Perhaps, for a while longer; but the name
as such is secondary. God reveals himself through historical, secular
events, and the meaning of the name given him will reflect the

cultural and historical setting of the age that names him. The technopolitan culture of the secular city may well have to find a new name for God. The Israelites, for example, went through many stages in naming God: from *El Elyon* to *Elohim, El Shaddai* and *Yahweh,* not to mention the much later *Adonai,* still used in synagogues. These names could serve as designations for successive periods of Israel's entire history. In any event, there is no point in making a fetich of the name. Besides, there are many other things of more direct bearing on the Christian's conduct, such as love and obedience. These precede the gift of tongues. We can rest assured that

> the man who is doing what God intends him to do at the place he intends him to be will be supplied with the proper words (p. 224).

The Sources of Secularization

Cox not only describes the secularization process as it is now going on but also traces its sources, as he sees them. In fact, he does this in his first chapter, "The Biblical Sources of Secularization." As the title suggests, Cox finds the sources in the biblical message itself, in the "impact of biblical faith on history." Presecular or primitive man lives in a world dominated by magic, which is more than an aspect of primitive life. It is the whole outlook, "a world view."

The Hebrew idea of Creation — the things created, not the act of creation — signals a radical and decisive turn in human history. Not only does it separate nature from God, but it also distinguishes man from nature. Here, then, is the beginning of the de-divinization process, of the *disenchantment* of nature, not in the sense of disillusionment but as implying "matter-of-factness." In Genesis the sun, the moon, the stars, the earth and the seas are not semidivine or divine beings but creations of Yahweh. None of them can claim religious worship. Cox, in one of his paradoxical twists, characterizes the creation narrative of Genesis as a form of "atheistic propaganda," in so far as it denies the magical and semidivine vision of the natural world. Nature is not to be worshiped or bowed to in adoration. Not to be venerated, it is also not to be ravaged but to be worked, directed and transformed by man. Man, in short, is given charge of nature, and what is described as its de-divinization or de-sacralization comes specifically from the Judeo-Christian representation of nature. But the point is that this representation is what fathered and now feeds the secularity of the city of man.

Moreover, the Sinai Covenant began the de-consecration or secularization of ethical values. Cox refers this effect to the prohibition against idols, "gods" fashioned by man. According to the mentality of ancient peoples, gods and value systems and religious worship were the same thing, indistinguishable and inextricable. Hence, in interdicting the "gods" the Sinai Covenant eliminated the divine element from religious and moral values and from their representations, so far as they were human projections, "the work of man's hand," reflecting social and historical conditions. In effect, the commandment against idols and idolatry "relativized" every human religious or moral conception. For, the reason given the Hebrews for the interdiction was not that *their* conceptions were good but that the true God is by his very nature beyond human conception and human replication.

The Bible is also a most ancient source of de-sacralization in the realm of politics — in the non-partisan sense, of course. The focal point in this regard is the Exodus, the effect of which was to turn the political order completely around. In Cox's succinctness, "No one rules by divine right in secular society. In presecular society, everyone does" (p. 22). Primitive peoples usually tend to identify the political order with the religious order. The political community (tribe, state, empire) acquires a religious role and responsibility. In rebelling in a body and departing from Egypt, the Hebrews dissociated Yahweh from the established sacral-political order and adopted a nonsacral conception of political rule. Christians at the time of Rome took a similar stance. They prayed for the emperor but would not burn incense on his altar, which was in effect to "deny him any sacral-religious authority."

Admittedly, "remnants and residues" of sacral politics survive. The Archbishop of Canterbury still crowns the king or queen of England *Defensor Fidei,* defender of the faith. In America priest, rabbi, minister intone prayers at the inauguration of the President. A quasi-sacral state prevails in Spain and some small Asian countries, e.g., Nepal. Paradoxically, Nazism in Germany, Fascism in Italy and the Stalinist cult of personality represented relapses into sacral politics. But the main trend is toward more de-sacralization, and no significant reversal seems likely. As far as Christianity is concerned, this is all to the good.

IV

The Era of De-sacralization

A number of authors calling for a "religionless Christianity" have met with considerable success. However, the success is not all attributable to the authors themselves. A religionless Christianity, so-called, appeals to certain groups because it fits in with a much larger movement, commonly designated by the rather ill-defined term "de-sacralization." Various studies of the movement have appeared in recent years. In the present chapter we shall deal with it, not in any exhaustive manner but only so far as it pertains to the burden of our study, namely the alleged opposition between faith and religion.

The Central Theme of De-sacralization

A close examination of the objectives of de-sacralization, its basic theme and purpose, should begin with the latest dictionaries and encyclopedias which deal with such matters. As regards individual authors, as early as 1953 Friedrich Gogarten suggested that secularization was the destiny of the age, a "chance" that should be made the most of.[1] Others have attempted to clarify the general idea of de-sacralization or secularization.[2] But when it comes to elaborating specific aspects or the position of individual authors and the present directions of the movement, not a great deal of literature is yet available. We do have, among others, a study of this sort by J. Sperna Weiland, a Reformed Church pro-

---

1. Friedrich E. Gogarten, *Verhängnis und Hoffnung.* Die Säkularisierung als theologisches Problem. Stuttgart, F. Worwerk, 1953. New edition, München, Siebenstern-Taschenbuch Verlag. 1966.
2. F. Delekat, *Über den Begriff der Säkularisation,* Heidelberg, Quelle &

fessor at the University of Amsterdam,[3] and Thomas W. Ogletree's contribution to the "death of God" debate.[4] The movement concerns not only dogmas and dogmatics but christian ethics as well. This has been clearly shown by the Dutch Redemptorist, C. van Ouwerkerk.[5]

As intimated, within the milieu that created the term "de-sacralization" it is currently enjoying great popularity, and while it may not be on everybody's lips, it is far too much the vogue to be ignored. Some may suspect that the appeal is due to the very vagueness of the idea it is meant to convey. Yet that would be oversimplifying the matter. One thing, in any case, is fairly obvious. Many contemporary minds find the term well-suited to describe the widespread belief, or at least the widespread hope that christian life and thought is moving in the direction of the "profane," the "secular," the "laical," as opposed to the "sacred," the "religious," the "clerical."

De-sacralization envisages the reinforcement — invigoration, vitalization — of temporal values, which are not simply to be tolerated but definitely "pushed," constructively however. It calls for the advancement of whatever pertains to man: his work, his science and art, his recreation and leisure, in short, this earthly existence all around. It summons man to greater knowledge and greater acknowledgment of "earthly realities," of their authentic meaning and purpose, their own substantiality, and goodness and truth, their own laws and rightful claims. De-sacralization wants man to be taken seriously: man, his world, its history. Its goals, it insists,

---

Meyer, 1958.

M. Stallmann, *Was ist Säkularisierung?*, Tübingen, Mohr, 1960.

M. Krinkels, "Sekularisering. Een poging tot begripsverheldering," *Theologie en Zielzorg*, 62 (1966), pp. 265-274.

3. *Oriëntatie. Nieuwe wegen in de theologie*[2]. Baarn, Het Wereldvenster, 1967.

4. *The "death of God" Controversy*, London, 1966.

5. Coenraad van Ouwerkerk, C.Ss.R., "Secularism and Christian Ethics," *Concilium*, vol. 25, pp. 97-139. [The English edition of *Concilium* is published by Paulist Press, New York, N.Y. / Glen Rock, N.J., 1964.]

are perfectly sound, its hopes and expectations perfectly reasonable, especially in the light of what 20th century man has already a-chieved. Henceforth, there are virtually no limits to what man can bring about, however incredible or fantastic it may have seemed in the past.

The movement, we have said, seeks a "reinforcement." This means different things to different groups. For some it means tell-ing the world anew of the intrinsic worth and dignity of human toil, of the value of man's technology. Others take it as a manifesto for humanistic atheism, or as an endorsement of absolute auto-nomy for this world rather than just a determination to procure earthly realities their proper recognition without the denial of other-worldly reality. The one thing that all agree on is the resolve to defend and promote every human good.

The partisans of de-sacralization are aware that it will take great effort to realize their purposes. But they are determined to let no difficulty stand in the way. They are prepared for obstacles, some of which are inescapable, e.g., the limits of man's knowledge and the risks inherent in any human undertaking. They know this and accept it, but not without doing their utmost to reduce the limits and the risks. There are, however, obstacles which seem to have no validity, which in their opinion are an undue hindrance to the legitimate promotion of the things of this world. These they are determined to meet head-on, to attack unceasingly until they are demolished or destroyed. Here is where the confrontation occurs, where the demand for de-sacralization arises. For among unnecessary obstacles not a few spokesmen would place religion or religions and the presuppositions thereof: God, the Bible, the Church, etc.

As mentioned a few moments ago, proponents of de-sacraliza-tion are in agreement as to the general purpose of the movement, which is vague enough to admit of a diversity of positions. Yet, even its general formulation should command the serious attention of those who come under attack or criticism, for it challenges Christians to re-examine christian life and thought as it developed through the centuries. As for particular schools, of these there is a great variety, ranging from one extreme to another, from minimal to maximal, from timid linguistic efforts (e.g., showing that "contempt" of the world does not really mean contempt after all) to all-out campaigns against a transcendent God who is nevertheless present in the world and in close relation with man. Between the extremes, between the advocates of a "mini-aggiornamento" and the prophets of the "death of God," [6] dwells an array of more or less far-out defenders of a "de-sacralization" of human existence. In the few pages that follow we speak only of those forms of this "indictment of the sacred" which seem to us to have merit, some more some less. We also consider some problems that must be faced and take note of such criticism as seems just. In addition, we suggest some clarifications which, possibly, may lend guidance to those whom the movement leaves in a state of confusion. All in all, there may be a case for some updating through de-sacralization. If so, we shall try to deal with it deservedly.

The "religious" obstacle against which de-sacralization is directed assumes various aspects, which are defined, more or less, by the various terms that are so freely tossed about. Some terms con-

---

6. In its April 8, 1966 issue *Time* magazine blazons the whole front cover with three words, Is God Dead? and on pp. 82-87 reviews the crosscurrents of reaction of American theologians to the challenge which the question implies and which has been stated most effectively by the following spokesmen of the "death of God" movement: J. J. Altizer (born in 1927, Methodist, professor at Emory University, Atlanta), William Hamilton (born in 1924, Baptist, professor at Colgate-Rochester Divinity School), and Paul M. van Buren.

Altizer is perhaps best known for his *Mircea Eliade and the Dialectic of Sacred* (Philadelphia, 1963) and *The Gospel of Christian Atheism* (Philadelphia, 1966).

Hamilton is author of *The New Essence of Christianity* (New York, 1961) and in collaboration with Altizer has also published a collection of articles titled *Radical Theology and the Death of God* (New York, 1966).

Van Buren has contributed *The Secular Meaning of the Gospel: Based on an Analysis of Its Language* (London, 1963).

vey the intention to be rid of an obstacle as though of a kind of servitude. In general de-sacralization, as we have said, is directed against everything classified as "sacred," which is to say everything that is the opposite of what the movement regards as the "profane." The term "religionless" in "religionless Christianity" is fairly clear, though it may not be the perfect adjective for what is meant. "De-clericalization" seeks in particular to prevent the "clergy" from assuming positions and functions that belong to the "laity." And, when the reference is to the Church in general as distinct from the world, we sometimes see or hear "de-ecclesialize" and, in some situations, "de-institutionalize."

Other terms have a more positive ring that suggests that the discussion has passed the polemical stage, terms like "secularization," "profanity," "laicality," etc. On the other hand, terms in *ism* — e.g., secularism, laicism — are studiously avoided, the reason being that *isms* often have undesirable connotations. Proponents, in other words, want to stress the worthiness of their cause, that it is good and just and sound.

Whatever the misgivings about de-sacralization, we should not jump to the conclusion that it is all a vast anti-religious plot. Doubtless, there is some of this in it, some anti-religious sentiment. That aspect of it may be left to others. We prefer to be guided by St. Paul's counsel to the Thessalonians: "Test all things; hold fast that which is good" (I, 5:21). As a matter of fact, and this is much more important, in the view of many if not most advocates de-sacralization is justifiable on christian grounds. Indeed, it is even said to be a distinctive mark of the christian revelation as compared with other religions. Be that as it may, de-sacralization does want to change, if not the face of the earth, at least the face of the world. Accordingly, we shall begin by taking a look at the face of the "image" of the world it wants to change, or from which liberation is sought.

"Sacral" vs. "Secular" Image of the World.

At a given turn in an evolutionary process whole origins are lost in the mist of time, a branch of living beings had arrived at the threshold of self-determination and the power of speech. From that moment on man, in proportion to his development, established a system of relations between himself and nature. This was not a thought-out or philosophically conceived system but one that grew out of his natural and instinctive behavior. Man, that is, had an experienced "image of the world," which as time went on and the image became clearer and clearer, he reduced to a logical system. The representations of the world proposed by modern philosophers are but expressions of the same image, albeit much enlarged and much refined.

Western man, at least in more recent times, is generally inclined to take a "dynamic" view of the universe as opposed to a "static" image. The static conception is attributed to Greek thought, which largely shaped the course of Western culture. A static universe is today as it was in the beginning, a universe established in the state in which we find it. For in the static world view the diversity of species is metaphysically determined, the laws of nature permanently fixed and the divisions of being eternally sealed.

The dynamic representation of the universe implies that life has not always existed on an even keel, on a plateau, but there have been "leaps" or "eruptions," sudden transitions from one phase or stage to another; and it also assumes that this will go on, that life will continue to have a "history," of which, moreover, life itself will be the "architect." Present-day scholars and researchers like to stress that this hopeful conception of "time" and progressive development is directly related to the genius of Semitic and christian culture.[7] Also, the idea of "dynamism" involves histori-

---

7. See Oscar Cullman, *Christ and Time;* trans. from German by Floyd Filson (London, S. C. M. Press, 1951). This work had an enormous influence in the French-speaking world. Also, Cl. Tresmontant, *Essai sur la pensée hébraïque*, Paris, Éd. du Cerf, 1953.

city as much as history, in fact more. History is largely out of man's hand; historicity is mostly his responsibility. Greek and medieval thought recognized history of a sort, viz. a succession of events occurring in a stable, unchanging world, immune to the evolutionary process. In the modern view the world itself is subjected to history because it is dominated by man, and not vice versa. The world is man's responsibility, its lordship is in his hands.[8]

Granted that there has been and will continue to be change and development in the world, in what direction is it going? Auguste Comte gives his answer in the "three-stage" theory of mankind. Man's development, in his view, goes through three stages: theological, metaphysical and positive [more popularly, "scientific"]. In the theological stage man seeks the essential nature of things, their first and final causes. The phenomena of nature are regarded as effects of the direct and continuous action of supernatural agents, whose arbitrary intervention explains the apparent deviations from the orderly course of the universe. In the metaphysical stage, which is basically only a modification of the first, supernatural agents are replaced by abstract immaterial powers, real entities implanted in every cosmic being which produce and account for all observable phenomena. In the third stage, the age of positivism, man finally recognizes his inability to attain the absolute knowledge he sought, the essential nature of things. Abandoning the effort to discover the origin and destiny of the universe, or the ultimate causes of natural phenomena, he dedicates himself to the study of the relationships between the phenomena and the laws that govern these relationships. This, in sketch, is the law of three stages that prevails in the development of mankind, a notion which Comte also applies to the individual. "Does

---

8. See A. Darlapp, art. "Historicité," *Encyclopédie de la Foi* (Paris, Éd. du Cerf) vol. 2, pp. 226-232, with a good bibliography. Also, Albert Dondeyne, *Faith and the World,* chap. 7, "Historicity," pp. 153-166 (translation of *La Foi écoute le monde;* Pittsburgh, Duquesne University Press, 1963).

not each of us," he asks, "have a recollection of having been a theologian in childhood, a metaphysician in youth and a physicist in maturity?" [9]

Comte's thesis has found support to this day. H. Urs von Balthasar finds the general idea acceptable, but with a proviso. The succession of three stages, he believes, should be incorporated into the more comprehensive notion of "perennial mankind" (*humanitas perennis*) — mankind viewed, presumably, as one man spanning the whole range of time up to the present.[10] From this standpoint each stage has a function that is neither absorbed nor replaced by the following. Each stage only manifests a different aspect of total man, a totality that requires that all aspects be somehow present at the same time. In other words, the succeeding stages of the totality are both old and new; something is retained and something surpassed. Granted these qualifications — and prescinding from other criticisms currently leveled against Comte's system — there is no gainsaying that man's primitive vision of the world is marked by a supernatural or superstitious relationship with nature, be it religious, magical, animistic or totemistic.

In time, namely when it is found that the cosmos is not under the domination of capricious deities but is governed by immutable laws, the primitive preternatural or magical relationship gives way to the philosophical conception. At this stage man's basic attitude changes as he contemplates what he believes to be "an ideal order realized in the universe [and adopts] a mode of action that will reflect and realize what has been experienced in the contemplation." [11] But man continues to explore the secrets of nature, and the more he explores them the more he masters nature and increases his technical and mathematical command of it. Therewith the third stage is born. Thoroughly in his power, man no

---

9. Auguste Comte, *Cours de philosophie positive*, Lesson 1.
10. Hans Urs von Balthasar, *Science, Religion and Christianity*, pp. 12-13; trans. of *Die Gottesfrage des Heutigen Menschen* by Hilda Graef (Westminster, Md., Newman Press, 1958).
11. *Ibid.*, p. 15.

longer regards the universe in a semi-religious light. Rather than knelt to, it now kneels to him, a pliant ward that man has the duty to command, to transform, to improve and render productive.

We have said (or as much as said) that the "theological" stage represents the age of primitive man, age of fables and myths. The point has not been lost on recent biblical scholarship. What if it should turn out that Sacred Scripture contains and proposes revelation in terms and categories that may have been relevant in a primitive age but today are definitely irrelevant and obsolete? If the exegetes are correct — the evidence is strongly in their favor — the Bible speaks, at least in part, through "mythical" conceptions of the world, which are alien to an age like ours where the scientific outlook prevails and the scientific spirit shapes the course of events. The "mythological" world view is behind us, for good. All in all, then, it was but a matter of time till someone would propose (and others fall in line with) a program for "demythologization" of the Bible.

In this respect, perhaps no one has done more nor is better known than Rudolph Bultmann, who does indeed personify the movement. The problem is to know where myth begins and stops. For Bultmann the part that is "myth" and therefore to be eliminated is a considerable amount. In the following passage R. Marlé summarizes his determination of mythical elements in the New Testament:

> The universe to which the biblical authors constantly refer is a three-tiered universe: the earth in the middle, heaven above, the nether world below; heaven as the habitation of gods and celestial beings, the angels; the nether world as hell, place of torment; the earth not as the place of natural day-to-day events, or place of provident care and toil, but as the stage where supernatural forces are the players, God and his angels, Satan and his demons. These forces intervene indeed in the course of nature but also in the life of man, in his thought and will and action, to the extent that miracles are a common-

place. Man is not his own master but can easily become a victim of possession by demons. Satan has the power to put evil thoughts into man's mind. But God also can bend the flow of man's thoughts and volitions, can make him have visions from above, make him hear his Word to inspire or comfort him, and impart to him the veritable power of his Spirit. History, for its part, does not follow a constant and regular course but receives its thrust and direction from supernatural powers.[12]

Bultmann's voice is not one that has fallen on deaf ears. Today the exegetical fraternity, almost to a man, is concerned with freeing the "pure revelation" from the incrustation that has made it obsolete and untenable. Then, and only then, will men of today have an authentic deposit of faith to stand on.

Here we should take a moment to consider the reasons that are given to justify this work of "reduction" or purification in regard to certain biblical narratives, viz., those that are presumably blended into a "world image" that modern man can no longer accept. For it is here that we are again confronted with the faith-vs-religion issue. In other words, it is precisely in the name of the christian revelation that the image of the world is adjudged too "religious" and therefore subjected to criticism. And it is in the name of the christian faith that the work of "demythologization" is undertaken.

It is said, for example — and quite rightly, of course — that the dogma of "creation" is of great importance for understanding the "created" world, in particular God's relation to man and man's relation to God. To be sure, there are those who would object that this is a pseudo-problem, because the Creator-God does not exist and the reality of the universe is the "total" reality.

---

12. R. Marlé, *Bultmann et la Foi chrétienne*, Paris, "Foi vivante," 1967, pp. 53-54. [Translation mine – Tr.] For a more detailed analysis, see IDEM, *Bultmann et l'Interprétation du Nouveau Testament*, Paris, Aubier, 1956 (2nd edition, rev. and enlarged, 1966).

Without God, then, our only concern is with the world and the things of the world. But the fact of the matter is that we do believe in a Creator-God, and this article of our faith (it is argued) is precisely the thing that bears out those believers who are advocating "de-sacralization." For the history of salvation begins with creation. Brought into existence by God were beings distinct from him. But by the very fact of making them distinct, he establishes himself in absolute transcendence relative to the created world. On the one hand, then, the created world is essentially dependent on the Creator, but it is also essentially and totally distinct from him. This explains (so runs the argument) why prophets of the Old Testament engaged in relentless attack against all religions, for religions jeopardize the transcendence of God. Nor did they spare the Chosen People when it succumbed to the like temptation, putting its trust in religion.

The dogma of redemption — some prefer "justification" and "sanctification" — is also cited in support of some "de-sacralization." For, with the God of Christians there is neither Jew nor Greek, neither slave nor freeman, male nor female, on the contrary "you are all one in Christ Jesus" (Gal. 3:28), baptized, justified, sanctified all, in him. The christian reality transcends the distinction of sacred and profane. It knows only one category, which has many names: redemption, justification, sanctification. This is the category that matters, that is radical, decisive, definitive. In this sense, and to this extent, the christian grace of sanctification has deflated the worldly pomp that clings to cults, to religions and to things sacred.

From considerations like these it is concluded that the Christian should adopt an "image of the world" that is nonsacred, nonreligious and secular. Too often, it is charged, he accepts, defends and propagates an image of the world that is "sacral" or, at the very least, "too religious."

The "Sacred"

We mentioned earlier that the term "de-sacralization" means different things to different people. Perhaps if we found a specific meaning for "sacred" we would be in a better position to analyze the movement that seeks to diminish the sacred. The dictionaries are not very helpful; variety of meaning abounds. Under "sacred" Lalande's *Vocabulaire* gives the following:

1) a strong and general sense: that which pertains to an order of things that is separate, reserved and inviolable; that to which religious respect is due on the part of the believer.

2) a moral and customary sense: the sacred character of a human person, a usage that also admits of the idea of absolute or incomparable value.

3) a weak and specialized sense: that which pertains to cult or worship, e.g., sacred music.[13]

A number of contemporary authors have attempted to determine the meaning of the term through the phenomenological and historical study of religious facts. Frequently mentioned in this regard are the investigations of Mircea Eliade, particularly *The Sacred and the Profane*,[14] and also the works of Roger Caillois, e.g., *Man and the Sacred*.[15] Jacques Grand'Maison's recent study of the question is excellent and should not only make sense to the general reader but also evoke response from university people.[16] Among other things, he points out that

some stand on the Latin meaning: *sacer,* inviolable; others trace the term back to the primitive Greek meaning, *hierax,* which has an a-religious content as compared with its derivative, *hieros.* Still others define the sacred in relation to the profane, *profanum,* vestibule of a temple or sanctuary. We be-

---

13. A. Lalande, *Vocabulaire . . . de la philosophie,* 9th ed., Paris, P. U. F., 1962, p. 937.
14. Trans. by Willard R. Trask (New York, Harper and Brothers, 1961). Also in paperback (Harper Torchbook 81, The Cloister Library, 1961). This work of Eliade is discussed later in the chapter.
15. *L'Homme et le Sacré,* Paris, Gallimard, Ist ed, 1939.
16. *Le Monde et le Sacré,* Paris. Éd. ouvrières, 1965.

lieve there is a danger in limiting the inquiry to the semantic level.[17]

Obviously, if "sacred" admits diversity so will "de-sacralization" — diversity as to meaning and interpretation, sources and research. In this multiformity of ideas and theories, however, some appear more prominent than others. Such is the theory of the "sacred" and the "profane" expounded by Emile Durkheim in *The Elementary Forms of the Religious Life*.[18] Consciously or otherwise, many proponents of de-sacralization, especially those who question the use of terms like "sacred" or "religion," have been influenced by Durkheim's analysis, the substance of which is stated in this passage:

All known religious beliefs, whether simple or complex, present one common characteristic: they presuppose a classification of all the things, real and ideal, of which men think, into two classes or opposed groups, generally designated by two distinct terms which are translated well enough by the words *profane* and *sacred*. This division of the world into two domains, the one containing all that is sacred, the other all that is profane, is the distinctive trait of religious thought. The beliefs, myths, dogmas and legends are either representations or systems of representations which express the nature of sacred things, the virtues and powers which are attributed to them, or their relations with each other and with profane things.[19]

What distinguishes these "sacred things" from "profane things"? There is nothing to define and differentiate them except their "absolute heterogeneity." [20] In all the history of human

17. *Op. cit.,* p. 25, note 11.
18. Trans. by Joseph W. Swain (London, George Allen & Unwin, n. d. New York, The Macmillian Co.).
19. *The Elementary Forms of the Religious Life,* p. 37.
20. The reference for this paragraph is *op. cit.,* pp. 38-39.

thought there "exists no other example of two categories of things so profoundly differentiated or so radically opposed to one another." The opposition between good and evil is "nothing besides this," for good and evil are "two opposed species of the same class, namely morals," whereas the sacred and the profane have always been conceived as "two worlds between which there is nothing in common." Admittedly, not all religions understand or interpret this opposition in the same way but "the fact of the contrast is universal."

And though it is possible for a thing to pass from one of these worlds into the other, this can only happen through a veritable metamorphosis, and that in itself "puts into relief the essential duality of the two kingdoms." [21] The initiation rites are a dramatic demonstration of the changeover. The passage from the profane world into the world of sacred things is thought of, "not as a simple and regular development of preexistent germs, but as a transformation *totius substantiae* — of the whole being." The young man dies, then is reborn. "Does not this prove that between the profane being which he was and the religious being which he becomes, there is a break of continuity?" So complete is the heterogeneity that it frequently degenerates into antagonism. The two worlds are not only conceived as separate realms but as "hostile and jealous rivals of each other." It is not possible to belong to one completely "except on condition of leaving the other completely." In some ways this is what happens in monasticism, which is "artificially organized" to create another environment, apart from and closed to the natural environment of men and "nearly its contrary." Briefly, then, what marks religious phenomena

is that they always suppose a bipartite division of the whole universe, known and knowable, into two classes which embrace all that exists, but which radically exclude each other. Sacred things are those which the interdictions protect and isolate;

---

21. For this paragraph, see *op. cit.*, pp. 39-40.

profane things, those to which these interdictions are applied and which must remain at a distance from the first.[22]

Durkheim is aware of the objections that might be raised against his theory, and lest the theory itself be misunderstood he is very explicit as to what it proposes:

> If, as we have sought to establish, sacred things differ in nature from profane things, if they have a wholly different essence, then the problem is more complex. For we must first of all ask what has been able to lead men to see in the world two heterogeneous and incompatible worlds, though nothing in sensible experience seems able to suggest the idea of so radical a duality to them.[23]

Derivable from this formulation of the problem is a particular conception of religion, which he defines as follows:

> When a certain number of sacred things sustain relations of co-ordination or subordination with each other in such a way as to form a system having a certain unity, but which is not comprised within any other system of the same sort, the totality of these beliefs and their corresponding rites constitutes a religion.[24]

For Durkheim, then, *religious* beliefs are representations which express the nature of *sacred* things as well as the relations which these things bear both to one another and to profane things. *Religious* rites, on the other hand, are rules which prescribe how to conduct oneself in the presence of *sacred* objects.[25]

Also receiving much attention today are, as previously indicated the works of Mircea Eliade, who has devoted himself to

---

22. The Elementary Forms of the Religious Life, pp. 40-41.
23. *Ibid.*, p. 42.
24. *Ibid.*, p. 41.
25. *Ibid.*, p. 41.

the phenomenological and historical study of religious facts. We have mentioned *The Sacred and the Profane,* written in 1956 and one of his better known titles. Discussed are such topics as "sacred space," "sacred time," "sacredness of nature," "sanctified life." [26] The Introduction lays down the general lines of the inquiry,[27] which differs noteworthily from another, much earlier and also much-renowned work, Rudolph Otto's *The Holy.*[28] Whereas Otto concerned himself almost exclusively with the nonrational aspect of religious phenomena, Mircea Eliade intends to grasp "the sacred in its totality." And he begins by defining it:

> The first possible definition of the *sacred* is that it is *the opposite of the profane* (p. 10).

Man takes note of the sacred because it "manifests" itself. Mircea Eliade's designation for this manifestation is "hierophany," which is

> the manifestation of something of a wholly different order, a reality that does not belong to our world, in objects that are an integral part of our natural "profane" world (p. 11).

Stone or tree, he explains, are not worshiped "in themselves," i.e., "as stone or tree," but because they manifest something "that is no longer stone or tree but the sacred, the *ganz andere* [wholly other]" (p. 12). Accordingly,

> by manifesting the sacred, any object becomes *something else,* yet it continues to remain *itself,* for it continues to participate

---

26. *The Sacred and the Profane.* For Translator, etc., see note 14 of this chapter. This work is cited from Harper Torchbook 81, the paperback edition.
27. Pp. 8-18.
28. Rudolph Otto, *The Idea of the Holy*; trans. by John W. Harvey (2nd ed., London, Oxford University Press, 1957).

in its surrounding cosmic milieu. A *sacred* stone remains a *stone* ... (p. 12).
Nevertheless, to those who have a religious experience,

all nature is capable of revealing itself as cosmic sacrality. The cosmos in its entirety can become a hierophany (p. 12).

Moreover, the man of archaic societies "tends to live as much as possible *in* the sacred or in close proximity to consecrated objects" (p. 12). For him the sacred is equivalent to power and therefore to reality in the truest sense. Which is to say that

the sacred-vs-profane polarity is often expressed as an opposition between the *real* and the *unreal* or pseudoreal (pp. 12-13).

By contrast modern man, through various influences, has de-sacralized the world and entered upon a profane existence. For him a meal is a meal, while for the "primitive" it can become "communion with the sacred," a "sacrament" (p. 17). We should realize, in other words, that

the *sacred* and the *profane* are two modes of being in the world, two existential situations assumed by man in the course of his history (p. 14).

These, then, are two possible frames of human existence. *The Sacred and the Profane* attempts to bring out the "specific characteristics of the religious experience," together with its many variations through the ages and its marked contrast with the profane experience of the world.

Mircea Eliade has made it plain what he sought to accomplish and what not. His intention, apparently, involved a value judgment. He states it as follows:

In comparing and contrasting the "sacred" with the "profane" we intended above all else to underscore the general impoverishment that has resulted from the secularization of a religious way of life. If we did not speak of what man has gained from the de-sacralization of the world, it was simply because that, we assumed, would be more or less common knowledge to our readers (pp. 9-10).

These lines, written in 1964, appear in the Foreword to the French edition. Mircea Eliade was truly aware that a movement toward de-sacralization was in progress and, in fact, says as much. His hesitation to address himself to it is understandable. For, as historian he felt it was not his part to lend himself to the turbulence of the day. But despite this reluctance he takes sufficient note of it to suggest three possible directions regarding the future course of the movement.

First, consideration might be given to all that is implied in the contemporary theologies regarding "the death of God." By acknowledging the radically profane character of the world and human existence we may find, or hope to find, that in this very condition lie the seeds of a new type of "religious experience," paradoxical as it may seem.

Or, a somewhat different point of view, we could take the position that "religiosity" constitutes an ultimate depth of human perception and awareness, one that does not depend on the historical and transitory distinction of sacred and profane and therefore does not necessarily disappear when "religions" disappear. Basically, then, the advent of the "profane" would represent a new manifestation of a primary quality of man that formerly manifested itself through the "sacred."

Lastly, we might simply refuse to admit that the distinction of sacred and profane characterizes religion, insisting rather that religion rises above "such a dichotomy of the real" (p. 11). Such, avers Mircea Eliade, is the case with Christianity. And there are those, he adds, who would go even further, "declaring that Christianity is not a 'religion'" (p. 11).

PART TWO

Horizons of Faith

Perhaps the best way to shed some light on the confrontation we are dealing with is to review what is meant by christian faith and christian religion, or the religion of Jesus Christ. In large measure the confusion that plagues many of the faithful today goes back to a doctrinal deficiency on their part. To be sure, they have some knowledge of the faith, and they deem it a blessing that there is a christian religion. Which is all to the good but hardly sufficient to ensure that they will not be troubled and distressed when they meet up with certain theological positions of our time.

In this section, then, we attempt to elucidate some of the more important aspects of the act of faith and to point out on what grounds the Christian teaching calls for a religion. We also try to explain in what way divine revelation bears on the activities of this world.

I

The Word of God and Man's Acceptance

Though we should like to begin here with extensive quotations from the dogmatic Constitution *Dei Verbum* (On Divine Revelation), our interests at the moment will be well enough served by the introductory statements of paragraphs 2 and 5.

2. In His goodness and wisdom, God chose to reveal Himself and to make known to us the hidden purpose of His will (Eph. 1:9) by which through Christ, the Word made flesh, man has access to the Father in the Holy Spirit and comes to share in the divine nature (Eph. 2:18; 2 Pet. 1:4).

5. "The obedience of faith" (Rom. 16:26, 1:5; 2 Cor. 10:5-6) must be given to God who reveals, an obedience by which man entrusts his whole self freely to God, offering "the full submission of intellect and will . . . ."
(*The Documents of Vatican II,* pp. 112, 113; New York, Guild Press, 1966. Angelus Book)

As companion material to our present topic we recommend that chapter 1 of the Constitution be read in its entirety.

The Word of God

The Word of God is God's act.[1] This act is absolutely gratuitous and supremely free. It is as transcendent as God him-

---

1. See *La Parole de Dieu en Jésus-Christ,* Tournai-Paris, Casterman, 1961;

self, transcending all created reality. It is always "actual," always present, even as God himself. And it is always "in action," for it expresses the mystery of the "living God." This "word" makes known the Lord God in the most universal manner.

Moreover, this Word is creative: "God said . . . and it was so" (Gen. 1). And it is prophetic, announcing and preparing the coming of the Kingdom of God: "The Lord has sent a word against Jacob, and it will light upon Israel; and all the people will know [its effects]" (Is. 9:8-9). And "revelatory," in the fullest sense: in the "word" the Lord reveals the reality of his love, communicates his thought, declares his might, unveils the mystery of his life and being. And salvific: at work and astir and in ferment in those who receive and accept it — activity which St. Paul expresses by the very meaningful word *energeitai* (I Thess. 2:13).

We have said that the word of God is operative and efficacious. "For as the rain and the snow come down from heaven, and return not thither but water the earth, making it bring forth and sprout . . . . So shall my word be that goes forth from my mouth; it shall not return to me empty, but it shall accomplish that which I purpose, and prosper in the thing for which I sent it" (Is. 55:10-11). If there is one property of the word of God — the "good news," as St. Paul has it — that is more prominent than others, it would be that it is "the power of God unto salvation to everyone who believes" (Rom. 1: 16). It is the "word of salvation" (Acts 13:26), "the word of life" (Phil. 2:16), "the word of grace" (Acts 14:3, 20:32). The word of God causes to happen what it asserts. "The words that I have spoken to you are spirit and life" (Jn. 6:64). According to St. John's writings the Word purifies and sanctifies, but it also judges and condemns, viz., those who will not re-

---

a collective work, presenting the various dimensions of the Word.
See also Otto Semmelroth, *The Preaching Word;* trans. of *Wirkendes Wort* by John J. Hughes (New York, Herder and Herder, 1965). Covers the theology of the Word of God.

ceive it. And St. Peter has this, "You have been born anew, not of perishable seed but of imperishable, through the living and abiding word of God" (I, 1:23).

The Word, in short, is not only the expression of a thought. It is also a sign of the will, a call, a command. It is charged with the power of him who utters it (Jer 1:9-10). It is an active power: the Lord watches over it to perform it (Jer. 1:12). Word of benediction, it brings what it promises. Word of malediction, it is not deprived of its effect. "The words that I say to you I speak not on my own authority. But the Father who dwells in me does his works" (Jn. 14:10).

God has spoken in many and various ways (Heb. 1:1). In times past, by the prophets — but also in the imperfect revelation vouchsafed to the great spiritual men of pagan religions. He spoke the word of promise to the Patriarchs, and the word of the Law engraved on tablets of stone on Sinai (Deut. 4:13). But more especially he spoke the word that welled up in the prophet and "lighted upon Israel" (Is. 9:7): word the prophet could not quell, much less originate, for Yahweh alone could engender it (Amos 3:8). Though a privileged messenger, the prophet had to pray and wait (Jer. 42:4, 7), a man of the Spirit (Hos. 9:7) yet not the source of the Word, only its herald and vehicle.

God now speaks to us by his Son (Heb. 1:1). Since the Incarnation the word of God is inseparably linked with the person of Jesus Christ: "And the Word was made flesh and dwelt among us. And we saw his glory . . . full of grace and truth" (Jn. 1:14). The Word incarnate reflects the glory of the Father and bears the image of his nature (Heb. 1:3). Jesus is the "Word of God," the creative thought of God, the creative utterance of God: "In the beginning was the Word, and the Word was with God; and the Word was God . . ." (Jn. 1:1-3). When the fullness of time had come, the "Word of Life" appeared. The disciples could hear it, see it, touch it, and they bore witness to what they had known, "the Eternal Life which was with the Father" (I Jn. 1-3).

After the Apostolic Age the activity and efficacy of the word of God continued. His word still revealed, still saved, and does today and without cease till the end. Even though interpretations vary, all Christians believe in the indefectibility of the Church. God has promised to be with the Church, to protect and assist it, till the fulfillment of the ages. Christians trust and believe that he will continue to save in revealing himself and to reveal himself in saving, namely through events in and out of the Church as time unfolds. His word is not spent, not exhausted, not dying.

Acceptance of the Word

Receiving and accepting the word of God is not a simple affair, easy to dissect and piece together again. If a poll were conducted among a Catholic community asking how they envision their faith in the word of God, in his revelation, we should doubtless get a great variety of answers, some stressing one thing, some another. Allowance made for whatever notional difference there may be, we could expect similar results with a Lutheran or Reformed parish. Much the same situation would be found in the history of christian preaching and theology. But why go to a parish? a school of preaching? a theological tradition? Why not go directly to the inspired writings, to the first christian "theologies," St. John's, St. Paul's, the Synoptics'?

The Pauline concept of faith comprises a "variety of psychological elements: desire, trust, obedience. These elements converge and anchor in the credence which the mind places in God or in Christ, credence by which faith is principally defined but by no means adequately covered." [2] We should never lose sight of this extraordinary many-sidedness of faith, of the New Testament *pistis*. Man uses more than one faculty in his theological activity, his relationship with God. Perhaps nothing illustrates this better in the christian life than the exercise of the virtue of faith with its manifold aspects, its formidable complexity.

---

2. *Dict. Théol. Cathol.*, vol. 8, col. 2063.

Faith, then, is a firm adherence to the person of Christ, Lord and Master; in other words, by faith we "receive" Christ — and receive him we must. Faith includes unyielding trust in his power: "O you of little faith, why did you doubt?" Faith drives out fear, for it gives us permanent access to the inexhaustible mercies of God. "Your faith has saved you." Faith is also submission to the word of God, of which the aforesaid Constitution takes note in speaking of the "obedience of faith." Through faith we experience God working in us, the divine life of grace. "The Spirit will teach you all truth." Through faith we have the confidence that causes prayer to be heard: "But let him ask with faith, without hesitation" (Jas. 1:6). "To believe *in* God," says Father Prat, "is not only to believe in his existence, but to rest *upon* him as on an immovable support, to take refuge *in* him as in a sure place of shelter, to tend *towards* him as to one's supreme end." [3]

Faith is reception of the salvific event, a *human* act. Faith is *eschatological* because of its orientation toward the end of time, the fullness of the Kingdom. And it has *historical* dimensions.[4]

A human act, faith is an act of the person. Faith — faith "alone," some Christians say — is the touchstone according to which we are favored with justification or, contrariwise, marked for rejection. Hence, every man is to be confronted with, and to face for himself, the act by which he would choose for Christ and decide to believe. This choice is born in the recesses of the soul. It is an act which combines freedom, love and knowledge in one, an act that takes place before the efficacious presence of

---

3. Ferdinand Prat, *The Theology of Saint Paul*, vol. 2, p. 238; trans. by John L. Stoddard (Collegeville, The Liturgical Press; London, Burns and Oates).

4. See the article "Faith" (with bibliography) by M. Seckler, Encyclopédie de la Foi (Paris, Éd. du Cerf) II, 140-162; J. Mouroux, *Je crois en Toi*, "personal" aspects of faith (Éd. du Cerf); R. Aubert, *Le Problème de l'acte de foi*3, Louvain, E. Warny, 1958 (presentation of the problem from the Middle Ages to the 20th century).

God who invites and summons. The "I" of man takes its stand as regards the "Thou" of God. Faith, accordingly, is a "personal encounter." Personal first of all because it is an act of the whole person, not of one faculty alone; personal also because it forms and enriches the person. Through the *metanoia,* the conversion that faith works in us, we acquire or begin to acquire that very manner of being man that Christ wills of us.

The call by which God invites us to share in his life represents first of all the a-conceptual manifestation and gift of himself. It is

> an ineffable communication of God in himself, not objectivized in representative content, but lived in the attraction of the transcendent toward himself. In response to this inner invitation man feels himself called to free acceptance of the absolute in his gratuitous self-giving, even though he has no reflective consciousness of this feeling. Man's free response (acceptance or rejection), anticipated and prefigured in his experience of this divine call, includes a true choice of faith, since man really accepts or rejects God who communicates and manifests himself in his attraction toward himself.[5]

To be sure, the choice man makes at this point does not yet possess the human fullness proper to the act of faith, for it does not involve conceptual expression of divine revelation. To this extent, then, the choice is still an incomplete act of faith, inasmuch as it does not achieve the full human affirmation of the content of revelation. But it is a choice, one that

> implies an embryonic faith, rooted in the ineffable depth of freedom — its exercise can transcend the conceptual knowledge that conditions this exercise — and not developed in the corresponding categorical expression; it is a faith that is lived,

---

5. Juan Alfaro, S.J., "The Dual Aspect of Faith," *Concilium,* vol. 21, p. 63.

but circumscribed (by circumstances outside the control of man's will), and one which will lead to conceptual assent.[6]

Faith is *historical*. The God of faith is a God who reveals himself in the history of a people in order to bring salvation to the world. The Bible contains the word of God but also — some would say "especially" — the deeds of God. The Word comes to us through men, hence through their words and deeds. These spokesmen or prophets were moved by the Spirit — "who spoke through the prophets," says the Creed of Constantinople. They told and sang the praises of the *mirabilia Dei,* the wondrous deeds wrought by God for Israel and all mankind. God intervened in the history of Israel. The encounter, the summons wakened Israel and won its love and devotion:

> Israel dwelt amid nature, but the focus of its attention was on *history*. What counted was less the annual cycle in which all things make a fresh start than what God *does, has done* and *will do* according to his promises. Promise and fulfillment, this was the dynamic factor in a time scheme of triple dimension. The present spills over into a future that was announced and promised in the past.[7]

Faith is historical for another reason: because it is "ecclesial." Christianity means "community." The encounter with Christ occurs in consequence of the Church's witness. It comes through her mediation and in the ecclesial environment which the Church creates. Hence faith walks close in hand with a tradition that nourishes its growth and regulates its vitality. Faith, moreover, is richly seeded with intimations from the Spirit and with suggestions of historical tasks which the Spirit invites believers to assume and engage in. If the word of God "begets the Church,"

6. *Ibid.*
7. René Latourelle, *Theology of Revelation,* p. 304 (Staten Island, N.Y., Alba House, 1966).

the Church in turn "presentializes" the word of God for men of every generation.

> Through the Church Christ calls every generation of men, announces to them his plan of salvation and urges them to be converted (Mk. 1:14-15). The Church, as Bishop Martin said at the first Vatican Council, is as though "revelation reified," *quasi concreta est revelatio* (Mansi, 51, 314B). Through the Church revelation is always present and always operative.[8]

Faith, finally, is historical in the sense that divine revelation also comes to us through universal history. This aspect of revelation is dear to many theologians today. However, theological development of it has only begun and needless to say calls for much discretion.

It is arguable that religious mystery is not only transmitted by the spiritual history of mankind but also, to some degree, revealed by it. In a letter in 1949 to Archbishop (now Cardinal) Cushing the Holy Office reminded Catholics that it is possible to be saved outside the visible Church, provided certain conditions are met.[9] But inasmuch as salvation is not possible without faith, one who is saved or justified must have received some revelation. God calls him, speaks to his inmost soul and inclines it toward the Trinity. And, as J. Alfaro explains, "By responding to God who reveals and gives himself, man in the last analysis is tending toward Christ, since God's revelation and grace coincide with the incarnation, which in itself contains the revelation and personal self-giving of God the Father to the man Christ, his Son,

---

8. *Ibid.*, p. 409.
9. See *Docum. Cathol.*, 1952, cols. 1395-1399.
   For a list of analytical articles on this question in general and on this letter in particular, see Boniface Willems, O.P., "Who Belongs to the Church?" *Concilium*, vol. 1, p. 138, note 20.

and in Christ to all men." [10] As a matter of fact, anyone who has been justified has also been admitted to the presence of the Kingdom, i.e., the Kingdom in mystery. This presence, hidden though it may be, is a source of spiritual abundance, even to such as know nothing of Jesus Christ.[11] All in all, there is reason to believe that at times the impulse, the inspiration and the spiritual illumination from God reaches the level of consciousness in religious souls throughout mankind, and that in this way the "Christian" revelation enters the "religious" history of the world.

But can it be said that so-called "profane" history also manifests God's will and purposes in the world? The question has been raised by H. Urs von Balthasar.[12] As he points out, no adequate judgment or evaluation of history can be made before the "free and definitive Word has been spoken" (p. 234). On the other hand, the Kingdom and the Judgment are already present in the world. With these eschatological realities in mind, what has to be considered is

the relationships between the Word and history as it affects the course of history itself. The lines along which such an investigation should be carried out may be seen from what we have already said, but they are not as narrow as many Catholics, influenced by Protestant theology, are inclined to think. The encounter between the Word and history can be made a matter of experience in two ways:

1. by detailing what the presence of the Word has produced and continues to produce in history and then, with these facts in hand, analyzing them for whatever message they contain;

2. by endeavoring, in the footsteps of the Fathers, to

---

10. *Art. cit.*, (note 5), p. 64.
11. See A. Röper, *Die anonymen Christen, Mayence*, 1962, pp. 80-136.
12. In the collective work *La Parole de Dieu en Jésus-Christ*, Casterman, pp. 227-240.

define and elaborate the total, perceptibly present salvation economy on the basis of the Word Incarnate's claim that his was to be a universal order of things, and also on the basis of his entrance and presence in human history (p. 235).

We shall come back to this point in chapter 3 of the present section.

Understanding the Word

Generation after generation, ever since the Apostolic Age, Christians have been busily trying to "understand" the word of God. The Lord, unfortunately, does not appear each time we have a difficulty to "interpret the Scriptures" (Lk. 24:27), as in the case of the disciples of Emmaus. But we are not without accredited "interpreters" and rules of interpretation. The aforementioned Constitution on Divine Revelation speaks to this point: "Since God speaks in Sacred Scripture through men in human fashion, the interpreter of Sacred Scripture, in order to see clearly what God wanted to communicate to us, should carefully investigate what meaning the sacred writers really intended, and what God wanted to manifest by means of their words." [13] To this end, continues the Constitution, it is necessary to have regard for the "literary forms" of the inspired writings and to pay "due attention . . . to the customary and characteristic styles of perceiving, speaking, and narrating which prevailed at the time of the sacred writer, and to the customs men normally followed at that period in their everyday dealings with one another." [14] What the Constitution is saying is that the inspired authors lived at a certain time and shared with their contemporaries the current image or picture of the world. This image enters into their writings and has a bearing on the meaning they intend to convey. Hence, to get at the real meaning of the revealed message it is

---

13. Constitution on Divine Revelation, par. 12 (*Documents of Vatican II*, p. 120; New York, Guild Press, 1966).
14. *Ibid.*

imperative to identify this image and to lift it, as it were, from the message itself: which is what "demythologizing" is about.

It follows, then, that some of "demythologization" is legitimate, necessary and timely. This is not to say, for instance, that Bultmann's criteria for separating message from "myth" must be accepted, but it is suggested that his efforts cannot simply be dismissed. Hermeneutics of the New Testament is a delicate problem, quite possibly the most delicate that theological science faces today. The message of the gospel was thought, conceptualized and formulated from a perspective of the world that differs sharply from ours, the perspective of scientific and technological man.[15] "We are fully persuaded," declared Pope Paul VI, "that bishops and priests cannot properly fulfill their mission of teaching and saving the world unless they are prepared to present, defend and explain the truths of divine faith in concepts and terminology that will be more comprehensible to minds formed by the contemporary philosophical and scientific culture." [16] This culture, obviously, is less "religious" than that of the New Testament authors.

Actually, we have already entered the age of "demythologization," an age in which efforts are being made to free revelation as such from the verbal and cultural dress, now variously outworn and outmoded, in which the inspired writers present it. All Christians know that much of Genesis need not be taken literally — nay, cannot be taken literally — and that the "reality" which is revealed was "narrated" after the manner of a primitive age. All Christians know, and have known for a long time, that "the substance of the prophetic message" must be found by removing it from a "triple wrapping: the wrapping of poetic images and symbols; the wrapping of literary themes borrowed from Israel's past and at times from the literature of neighboring nations;

---

15. See R. Marlé, *Bultmann et la Foi chrétienne,* Paris, "Foi vivante," 1967. This states the essentials of the contrast. For a more scientific presentation, see IDEM, *Bultmann et l'Interpretation du Nouveau Testament,* Paris, Aubier, 1966².

16. *L'Osservatore Romano,* French edition (July 22, 1966), p. 1.

finally and above all from the wrapping of expressions, ideas, images and types borrowed from the religious and historical environment, from the surroundings of nature, from the political structure, the Mosaic economy — from all those spheres of life and reality in which the prophets of the Old Law moved and exercised their ministry." [17]

So long as hermeneutics touches only inspired texts of the Old Testament, Christians are not apt to be greatly disturbed or to show much resistance. But today exegetical criticism is no less a questioner and overhauler of the New Testament. Naturally, the more extreme or unacceptable the hermeneutics that makes the press, the greater the jolt, especially among the faithful who read the Gospels as though they were historical writings as understood by modern scientific historians. Whatever the excesses of their fellow workers, the exegetes themselves may be counted on to handle that aspect of the problem. The faithful, for their part, could also and indeed will have to show some improvement in their attitude. They should recognize that even today, with all our means of information and communication and despite every effort to be perfectly accurate in everything pertaining to the inspired text, critics still discover gaps in the text, incorrect readings and even an occasional error. They should realize and reconcile themselves to the fact that the Gospels are not historical writings in the modern sense. An important Instruction issued by the Pontifical Biblical Commission April 21, 1964 deals with this very point.[18] Following are some passages which deserve the reflective attention of the faithful.

In composing them [the books of the Old and New Testament]

---

17. E. Tobac - J. Coppens, *Les Prophets d'Israel*, I, Malines, 1932, p. 72. It should be noted that this work is largely "pre-Conciliar" [scil. not only chronologically — Tr.].

18. *Instruction Concerning the Historical Truth of the Gospels*, trans. with commentary by Joseph A. Fitzmeyer, S.J., (Glen Rock, N.J., Paulist Press, 1964). [English citations are from this translation. The secretary of the Biblical Commission also issued an English version. It can be found, among other places, in *Catholic Biblical Quarterly* 26 (July,

the sacred writers employed the way of thinking and writing which was in vogue among their contemporaries (par. IV).

It would be gratifying if the faithful were to interest themselves in these modes of writing or narrative "forms" that were current (say) in the first century among Semitic peoples.

When the Lord was orally explaining his doctrine, he followed the modes of reasoning and of exposition which were in vogue at the time (par. VI).

How many of the faithful know anything about this Semitic mode of "reasoning" in vogue in the first century?

There is no reason to deny that the apostles passed on to their listeners what was really said and done by the Lord with that fuller understanding which they enjoyed, having been instructed by the glorious events of the Christ and taught by the light of the Spirit of Truth (par. VIII).

Perhaps it is not sufficiently appreciated that the "fuller understanding" which the apostles acquired consisted, in part, in the selection they made of things to be narrated. As the Instruction remarks, from the many things handed down the sacred authors of the Gospels

selected some things, reduced others to a synthesis, and still others they explicated as they kept in mind the situation of the churches (par. IX).

1964, 305-12), and *American Ecclesiastical Review* 151 (July, 1964) 5-11 — Tr.].

[On a more personal note, I am indebted to Father Anthony Leuer, St. Timothy's Church, Los Angeles for the loan of his English copy of the Instruction — Tr.].

Par. 19 (*Documents,* p. 124) of the Constitution on Divine Revelation is almost entirely a borrowing from this Instruction.

The Instruction means exactly what it says. The sacred authors made a choice, they summarized some of the things chosen and, perhaps most significant of all, they "explicated" or "developed" some others. In other words, they display considerable freedom in the handling of their material. The same freedom or latitude appears in the way they "narrate" the things they had witnessed. For, not only did they select

> the things which were suited to the various situations of the faithful and to the purpose which they had in mind, [but they also] adapted their narration of them to the same situations and purpose (par. IX).

In line with this, the Evangelists narrated the words and deeds of our Savior in different contexts, depending on the particular purpose they had in presenting them. This does not discredit their accounts, for

> the truth of the story is not at all affected by the fact that the Evangelists relate the words and deeds of the Lord in a different order, and express his sayings not literally but differently, while preserving the sense (par. IX).

We should not overlook the contrast here made, viz., "letter" versus "sense."

The exegete, continues the Instruction, must take into account everything that pertains to the origin and composition of the Gospels and put to proper use the discoveries of research. Otherwise he will not fulfill his task, which is to know what the sacred writers intended and what they really said. The faithful, too, should be informed about these matters if they would truly know and ponder what the Evangelists intended to transmit to the Church.

Finally, it might be asked if there is a connection between hermeneutics and "de-sacralization." The answer is definitely yes. We have said that in his teaching Jesus followed the "mode of thinking" of his time and the inspired authors the "mode of thinking" of their time. This means that to some extent, at least, they accommodated the preaching of the christian message to the current "world image," which was certainly more "religious" than ours. It is in this accommodation where hermeneutics and de-sacralization meet, with varying results but not necessarily bad.

II

Christian Faith and Christian Religion

Christian faith, it has been said, ought to replace religion. As a matter of fact, religion can be defined in a way that makes this statement acceptable. But it is much more accurate to say that the christian message comprises values that can be called "religious," that the christian faith naturally assumes "religious" form and expression, and that in this sense and to this extent the New Testament has laid down the general lines of a religion.

Content of the Christian Message

If we examine the writings of the New Testament and the lives of those great spiritual men who were inspired authors, we find that the terms *faith* and *to believe* are used in two ways. In the one case they refer directly to Jesus, to Christ, to the Son of God, to God. In other instances they relate to a doctrinal proposition that clarifies or details the content of revelation: "We believe *that* you are the Son of God."

Primarily, the act of faith envisons a reality: God the Savior. Faith means living with God, with the Lord. "Ultimately, the act of faith has to do not with a proposition but with a reality." [1] But faith also addresses itself to a message. It has doctrinal content: the gospel, the kerygma. All Christians admit that certain doctrines and precepts, certain rites and some sort of ministry are indispensable to a Christianity or a Church that claims to be "christian," to be "of Christ." These things, in other words, have been willed and instituted by Jesus Christ, though the extent

---

1. Thomas Aquinas, *Summa theol.* IIa, IIae, q. 1, a. 2, ad 2m.

of his institution has to be determined. It is by his will that they are constitutives of the Church, essential and necessary so that without them the Church neither would nor could exist. That among Christian Churches there is some disagreement as to what is "of divine institution" is beside the point. No Christian Church would dare to deny that there is a basic creed of the christian faith, that there are commandments of the Lord, and certain rites by which the Church is constituted (such as baptism and the Lord's Supper), and an authorized christian ministry.

Obviously, these things have to do with the justification of believers in Christ. But they are also connected with the praise and glory and adoration that believers are called upon to render to the one Lord. Catholics, of course, insist rather strongly on the importance of "mediatory" realities. For them, the sacraments "contain" the grace that comes from God. Yet among Protestant or Reformed Christians even those who preach a very energetic — though not extreme — version of the "actualist" or "social" gospel, even they acknowledge that at a given moment the bread, the wine, the water, the preaching are "signs" of the efficacious Word, so that at that moment at least they partake of the order of things by which man is sanctified and he who alone is Lord is glorified.

Christ's institution of the visible, sacramental economy of the New Testament was not haphazard or arbitrary. This economy is a "body" of realities, a "coherent order of things," the visible texture of the Church. And these "means" of sanctification and glorification, taken together and in their organic unity, are the Church in her capacity as "institution" of salvation, as "ordinary means of salvation." [2] This, to be sure, is not the only aspect of the Church of Christ, however formative and essential it may be. For the Church is a communion, a living organic totality, and though it possesses the aforesaid visible form and fabric, it is also, indeed *primarily,* the christian assembly in spiritual and living union with the risen Lord. This, in fact, is the heart of the

---

2. Denzinger, *Enchiridion,* no. 3869.

Church, that which is best, which is first and last and, in view of its eschatological promise, forever. Pending the "time of the Church," — the Church on earth, obviously — the whole purpose of the aforementioned visible realities is to serve the community of Christians, community of faith and brotherly love.

But a community of men cannot really "live" all the realities proposed to it by Christ if it accords them only the absolute minimum as regards implementation or manifestation and expression. Demanded, on the contrary, is a certain amplitude, expansion in space, extension in time, in short, a "size" of one kind or another. These realities have to have lodging not only in the interior man (in his consciousness, love, thoughts, meditation, symbols, mental images). They also require location outside (in rites, assemblies, fixed times, fixed places — whether for the once or lastingly doesn't matter). Strictly speaking, of course, these externalities are not of divine institution. But trying to do without them is simply to close one's eyes to the human condition as it actually is.[3]

The need for "size," for "spread" in space and time, stems not from something foreign to Christianity but from the very "means" of sanctification and glorification: profession of faith and commandments, sacramental actions, various functions of the ministry. There needs to be a certain solemnity to the profession of faith, a spiritual environment to the rites and ceremonies, a general furnishing for the functions of the ministry. All Christians know and accept this, even if all do not construe it in the same way.

These "means" exist in order that the faithful, here and now might "live" in "theological" communion with God. But that implies that we obey the word of God. And if we are going to obey it, we must first hear and understand and accept it. And that presupposes preparation on our part. Preparing oneself: this involves ascetical practice, regularly and not by fits and starts. Hearing the word: not merely from the pulpit on Sunday morning

---

3. Actually, i.e., before the Parousia.

but in the privacy of the soul, in meditation and recollection. Accepting the word: by responding to it with love of God and love of neighbor, a never-ending pursuit. The point is that "life" in the Spirit does not renounce external human actions and attitudes. To express itself properly it needs "room," i.e., any number of conditions and adjuncts of the spatial and temporal order. There are those who are concerned with creating in the Christian a theological relationship that is "pure," an appreciation of the transcendent that is "pure," yet seem to have no appreciation or regard for the conditions that are necessary to make this possible. The so-called "theological life" cannot exist in a vacuum. The human condition must be considered as it is now, during the "time of the Church." And this, it seems, is precisely what is often overlooked. The "parousia" will no doubt effect some alteration in the human condition, but there is nothing to suggest it has arrived.

Frankly, seeing the criticisms of certain Christians in regard to the "means of sanctification" or (to use their belittling description), "helps of the institutional order," a person could easily get the feeling that perhaps they are suffering from a slight case of "cerebral deficiency," forgetting that they are still "wayfarers" living in the "time of the Church," and not in eternity. No one questions that living the "theological" dimension of the christian faith is imperative, or that "ecclesiastical means" are just that — means. But it is significant that many times those who are making a "real" effort to live the "theological" dimension of the christian life are also the ones who frequent — with renewed spirit and enhanced appreciation — the sacraments and church services, in a word, the well-known "means of salvation." Good sense would seem to indicate that these are the persons in whom to put one's trust and confidence. Also, many priests can testify to this: that those who have lost the habit of living the "theological" dimension quite often attribute it to having lost contact with a church, an observance or some other element of the institutional order. Testimony like this cannot be dismissed with a snap of the finger.

Sacred Realities and Means of Sanctification

No doubt the reader will say that what we have been discussing sounds like "religion," like things "sacred." Quite so. But we have now to see how these terms apply on two different levels, that of creation and that of redemption.

Speaking of the creational level, C. Geffré declares that "through the mystery of creation there is already a *sacred* element at the root that coincides with the 'truth' of the world as such in itself." [4] This sacred, he continues, "is in the nature of a relationship, and that is why it does not jeopardize the solidity and autonomy of the profane." On the contrary, it "demands and provides a basis for it [the profane]. The things that express this "creational sacred," viz., beliefs, precepts and rites, could be called "religion." As for the economy of redemption, it requires — and the requirement in this case is even stronger — activities of the visible, human order and therefore inscribed in a given time, at a given place. These activities exist "alongside" those which constitute the regular occupations of men and, in contrast to the sacred, are referred to as "profane" or "secular." This, in essence, is Geffré's position. Our attitude toward it will be more or less apparent from what follows.

The history of salvation begins with creation, and the fact of creation has considerable bearing on the problem under discussion. For, when God creates, the things created are distinct from him. By creating them distinct — he could not do otherwise — he establishes his absolute transcendence in regard to them. The creature, then, is essentially dependent on the Creator and just as essentially and entirely distinct from him.

By the divine act of creation, "extra-divine" reality comes into being. "Since the creature is not divine but is something new and different, it must have its own being." [5] God is infinitely different from his creation. He and his creation could not possibly form one

4. "De-sacralization and the Spiritual Life," *Concilium,* vol. 19, p. 120.
5. H. Volk, "Creation," *Encyclopédie de la foi* (Paris, Éd. du Cerf) I, 299-300. Citations in this paragraph are all from this source.

and the same being. "In the creature nothing is divine, in God nothing is creature. Hence the creature has being and content so proper to it, so much its own, that theology by itself cannot give a complete account of it." There does indeed exist some relation between God and the creature, but his relation is not the whole being nor even the strict essence of the creature. Hence it is possible, in fact necessary, to make "nontheological affirmations" concerning the creature.

Yet despite the infinite difference and distance between the creature and the Creator, no creature is a stranger to God. On the contrary, "every creature is variously related to its Creator, and these relations determine beyond recall the essence and reality of the creature. In consequence of this determination theological affirmations about everything that is not divine become not only possible but necessary. In fact, the theological conception of created reality can be developed to a point where it permits us to see the ultimate ground for the irrevocable and determinative relations that exist between the created and the Creator yet do not compromise either the reality that is the creature's or the reality that is the Creator's."

In more formal terms, to be a creature means to be a finite or limited participation in the infinite or unlimited being of God the Creator:

> If God creates beings which are distinct from himself, these creatures must be finite or limited participations of his Infinite Being. He cannot create an infinite being, another "himself," since it is contradictory that there be several infinities. God can be participated in only by finite beings.[6]

The creature's basic relation to God is one of dependence, and this has profound implications for man. It is a "transcendental" relation, not in the Kantian sense but in the sense that though it is

---

6. F. van Steenberghen, *Ontology*, p. 232; trans. by Martin J. Flynn (New York, Joseph Wagner - London, B. Herder, 1952).

not strictly the essence of the creature it is nevertheless inseparable from the creature's being. We believe the relation should be of concern to those who deny God's existence as well as to those who affirm it.[7] Man can take cognizance of it, accept and acknowledge and ponder it. And it can move him to reflect on what he is, his ultimate nature and reality. He can also express the acknowledgment of this relationship of dependence in visible manner, viz., through acts of worship and praise. He can emerge from himself to form a community with others and thus begin to establish a "cult" of ritual worship simply on the basis of his creatural condition. Inevitably, he will then turn to created realities for ways and means of expressing his worship. He will employ symbols, actions and attitudes, signs, objects. Objects especially can become signs and symbols when man uses them to express his interior worship. They can also be set aside for occasions when men want to give more explicit, more complete acknowledgment of their creatural condition and thereby of their Creator.

We spoke earlier of Durkheim's conception of the "sacred" and "profane." The conception has many followers, or at least many for whom it is a point of reference for their thinking. Some Christians, however, would hesitate to apply the term "sacred" (as opposed to "profane") to the "creational" relation or to whatever expresses or conditions it. The relation between the created and the Creator is a relationship of total dependence, and this dependence applies to every creature, "profane" and "sacred." Moreover, this same created being, precisely as part of the world and the universe, is totally being, a being endowed with its own reality, its own specific laws and therefore its own autonomy. It follows, then, that Durkheim's sacred-vs-profane concept is not exactly the same

---

7. "Insofar as every spiritual perception and freedom constitutes a 'transcendental experience' on the side of the subject and his act, i.e., an experience of the unbounded orientation of the spirit to being in general, there is, on the part of the subject, in every perception a real, though implicit, i.e., not necessarily objectively realized, perception of God" (K. Rahner, "What Does Vatican II Teach About Atheism?" *Concilium*, vol. 23, p. 17).

thing as the creature-creator relation that appears in the christian revelation. Consequently, those who wish to apply the Durkheim antithesis to this relation should realize that they have to dissociate themselves from his theory and make clear what they are about.

There are, however, other definitions of the sacred besides Durkheim's. As we saw earlier, Lalande gives several meanings, one of which conveys the idea of "absolute, incomparable value." If this is how C. Geffré understands it, we can see why he would speak favorably of the "original *sacred* that coincides with the truth of the world." On the other hand, Lalande's illustration of this meaning, viz., "the sacred character of the human person," should not go unnoticed. Granted that this is a legitimate acceptation of "sacred," it will need considerable refinement before it can be applied to the "uniqueness" of God the Creator or to the transcendental relation between the creature and the Creator.

Concerning the economy of redemption the question before us is whether the salvific act by which we are justified in the Spirit of the Lord should be called "religious" or "sacred." Or does the christian dispensation prefer a different term, and what would it be?

The inspired authors speak of justification and sanctification in one and the same breath. Moreover, the Lord is chiefly the Holy One, holy beyond compare. "You alone are holy" (Gloria). Consequently, we can feel quite free to give the preference to the category of holiness. Support for this view comes from the Constitution *Lumen Gentium*.

> Christ, the Son of God, who with the Father and the Spirit is praised as "uniquely holy," loved the Church as his bride, delivering himself up for her. He did this that he might sanctify her. He united her to himself as his own body and brought it to perfection by the gift of the Holy Spirit for God's glory. Therefore in the Church, everyone whether belonging to the hierarchy, or being cared for by it, is called to holiness, . . . this holiness of the Church is unceasingly manifested, and

must be manifested, in the fruits of grace which the Spirit produces in the faithful (no. 30).

Practically speaking, all Christians recognize that the pre-eminent category is holiness. The reasons for it may not be clear to them, but they know it to be true. All Christians know that if a consecrated or "sacred" person is not in the state of grace, he is shunned by God and in danger of eternal damnation. They likewise know that if a "profane" or "secular" person — baker, geologist, shoreman, ad infinitum — is in the state of grace, living by the teachings of the Lord, he will be blessed by God and assured of glorious resurrection. Christians, that is, realize that from the standpoint of the christian faith the categories "saint" and "sanctification," and their opposite "sinner" and "damnation" transcend and overshadow the antithetical distinctions "sacred-vs-profane" and "religious-vs-nonreligious." This point is of great importance. It is receiving much attention today and Christians should mark it well. For even though some may feel that it is necessary at a certain stage of christian existence to maintain the distinction of "religious" and "nonreligious" or "sacred" and profane," this stage represents a secondary phase in the economy of salvation and is destined to pass away.

The same question arises concerning places of prayer and worship, articles and materials for the sacraments, the person of the ministers, priests and clerics in general, etc. Ought we to speak of them as "sacred" or "religious"? And then, in what sense?

An altar, a chalice, a church can be put to different use and become a table, a drinking cup, a dwelling. Their so-called "sacred" character does not change their basic nature. The blessing or consecration of a church, a liturgical rite ratifying the use of the structure for worship only, results in no change in its physical condition. Like any other building, it has to be kept in repair, and who knows but what some day it will become a museum? Even at the Eucharistic worship, the central action of the christian dispensation, the "species" of bread and wine retain their physico-chemical structure.

Until now these objects and places have generally been named "sacred" or "religious." Offhand, this seems proper and appropriate. Nevertheless it conceals a real danger. If some objects and places and persons are called sacred or religious, what is more natural than to conclude that other persons and created things are "nonreligious" or "nonsacred." As a matter of fact we name them accordingly, using the terms "profane" and "secular." The succession of contrary movements and ideas is not unusual. History, that of Christianity and its spirituality included, is full of examples. But the question is whether this division of created reality into two groups, one sacred the other profane, one religious the other nonreligious, is strictly in harmony with the christian revelation. Is it not perhaps a regrettable survival, within Christianity, of categories that pertain to other religions or to the sociology of religion? In any event, serious consideration might well be given to the proposal to emphasize the category of holiness and to promote it above all others.

To this end we might give some thought to the way we refer to the christian ministry. Instead of characterizing it as sacred or religious, perhaps we could speak of it as "ministry of sanctification," which would include persons and (by way of corollary) objects, places of prayer and worship. From this point of view everything, including the persons charged with the ministry, retains its proper being, identity and autonomy. If God's people are called to communion of life with the Lord, the Holy One par excellence, then its ministry is indeed a ministry of holiness or sanctification. Basically, this communion is realized in christian love, the theological charity, and in each one performing his duties of life. Communion in love is the bond of perfection and the fulfillment of the gospel. Charity characterizes the true disciple of Christ, and charity gives direction to the means of sanctification. Charity is their soul, their vital principle, and brings their purpose to fruition. If charity is to grow and prosper in the soul, it must be implanted in the organic totality of the means of sanctification, i.e., the gospel, the sacraments, the ministry, a totality whose doctrinal and ritual reinforcement pertains to the "ecclesial" order.

It is possible, then, to say a good deal in explanation of the christian faith without having to introduce the term "sacred," assuming that there really are some disadvantages to its use and that of its opposite, "profane." Those who maintain that the antithesis of sacred and profane is not a New Testament distinction or is not christian are to a large extent on solid ground, namely so far as in the New Testament the ideal of holiness transcends this antithesis and dominates and in a sense sublimates and surmounts its polarity. And, apropos of God, would "mystery of holiness" be less worthy than "sacred mystery"?

As for the term *religious,* do the same reservations apply to it? We think not. There is need, in other words, of a special term to designate the totality of created realities which form the spatial or human dimension of the "ecclesial" order. No man can do without this dimension if he truly acknowledges his condition as sinful creature reconciled by the Lord Most High. But if used, the term has to be strictly limited to what seems to be its etymological meaning, viz., "to bind again to the transcendent God." It must also be kept from encroaching on the category of holiness, with its absolute and universal pre-eminence in the christian scheme of reality.

III

Revelation and Active Presence in the World

The words of J. Mouroux concerning religious experience
may also be said of the christian faith, namely, that it is communitarian and it is active — and for several reasons: It is
communitarian

because man never stands before God except as member of
of an immense family; because the primordial attitude of all
true religion is embodied in the words "Our Father who art
in heaven"; because no one can seek and find God unless he
also helps others to seek and find him; because the more
a person discovers of the mystery of his God the more he
discovers of the mystery of a divine call that is also addressed
to others, to all others, a call that is as necessary in their
case and as individual as was his; and because no one can
dedicate his freedom to God without dedicating it to the
establishment of his kingdom and the promotion of his reign
among men.[1]

And faith is active,

because it is an involvement which, to be real, must uplift
human life, govern one's activity in the concrete and express
itself in specific undertakings.[2]

---

1. Jean Mouroux, *The Christian Experience*, p. 16; trans. by George Lamb
(New York, Sheed & Ward, 1954). [However, the translation of this
passage and the following one is my own, simply because the S & W
edition did not come to my attention in time — Tr.].
2. *Ibid.*, p. 16.

The Problem

If this is how matters stand between revelation and the world — in the sense of culture and civilization — will there be any relationships or common interests between them? If there are, where and how are they to be identified? In dealing with these questions it must be kept in mind that man's activity cannot be dissociated from the environment in which it takes place and which in turn it influences.

From the standpoint of revelation the development of the world and of human history is marked by a point of departure and a point of arrival, a beginning and an end. Chronologically, not to say spiritually and in many other respects, revelation takes us back to a beginning when the world was much as we know it. There is Light and there is Darkness. There is the ferment of life and the anguish of death. There is also a source of truest Life. At the end, at the completion, revelation envisions a world in which Light shall have triumphed forever, Life destroyed all death, and Glory obliterated all corruption: a world, that is, in which the Spirit shall be all in all. At that moment the reign of the Fatherhood of God over every creature will be perfect and perfectly complete. The presence of the Word made flesh will have perfect sway over this world and all that is in it. And the spiritualization by which the Spirit animates all things will have reached its perfect fulfillment. This world will then be perfectly "spiritual," hence perfectly "brotherly," hence perfectly "filial." Therefore, to make our world of today more "christian" means to help it to be more "spiritual," — now, from this moment.

In christian thought to be "spiritual" is to participate in the life of the Spirit, to follow the impulses and inspirations of the Spirit, to live according to the desires of the Spirit. It should be obvious that in actual fact and practice this does not assume the same form in every instance. It will vary accordingly as it pertains to an individual or group of individuals, to the Church as "ordinary means of salvation," or to the world in the sense of culture and civilization.

As regards the individual, when the Spirit dwells in a person he becomes, so to speak, the "soul" of the person's higher faculties, he "animates" them. Participating in the life of the Spirit, human powers are as though "fecundated" by the Spirit and so are "spiritualized" in the theological sense of that term.

In the case of the Church, we may apply the Lord's promise that "where two or three are gathered in my name, I am in their midst." If the presence of the Spirit is always efficacious, there is a special efficaciousness in the presence that pertains to the various means of justification and praise. This presence is associated with the word of God and the sacraments. As for other components of the Church, those properly human aspects which implement and express and nourish the theological life and the work of reconciliation, this is the area where the Church and the world come together, an area of joint interest.

Regarding the world and the Spirit: for the world to exist according to the Spirit means that, *before all else,* it functions and develops according to the norms that are *proper* to culture and civilization. To become "christian" and "spiritual," profane institutions — family, city, environment — do not have to be turned into mini-churches. Such an approach to the problem would be a gross mistake. Secular entities have their *proper* perfection, and it is important and imperative that this perfection be realized. Our task, then, is not to find religious or cultual substitutes for the world but to offer the world direction, to provide the "orientation" toward God as it pushes forward in the pursuit of its proper and fundamental perfection. Consequently, the ideal of making "spiritual" progress in a temporal vocation respects the autonomy and the identity of the world as such, the "profane" world. To say these things is to speak a christian tongue; it is to take a "christian" stance, yet a stance that is, *first of all and essentially,* "profane" and "laical" (and if it please) "nonreligious."

We have said "first of all and essentially," implying perhaps that there is more involved, more to be said about the world in relation to faith. But are there other considerations besides the world's own perfection? As far as the strictly "technical" or "scientific" world is concerned the answer can be no. Two and two always make four, and the state of grace does not alter physical or chemical laws. Hence, those whose concern is limited to the technical or scientific aspect of things — be it the world, civilization, progress, history, even culture — or who consider these things simply as products of science and technology have nothing or virtually nothing to add to what we have said regarding the christian stance toward the world, a stance which, as we have just seen is "profane" and "laical" or "nonreligious." This narrow view of the world, for so it seems to be, is observable in authors who keep wanting to know what should be the religion of the "modern" man, the "modern" city, the "modern" world. More often than not "modern" means "scientific" or "technological." But should it?

The world — culture and civilization — is more than a technological reality. It is basically "human," which is to say all its values are not of the quantitative order. It carries a qualitative dimension. It is tractable to the actions of free agents. Its destiny, then, is not completely dominated by inexorable laws. Conseqently, it would seem that a particular philosophy or conception of the world can influence its development and history. The christian faith has a definite view of the world, a *Weltanschauung,* that of revelation and of Jesus Christ. Some thirty years ago Max Lamberty published a Dutch work dealing with "domination and human distress" in recent European history.[3] The conviction carried away from this work is that the factors which determine the course of history are not all economic or scientific, that man's view of the world also plays a role. There is no reason why the christian view would be an exception, why it would not be a comparable influence.

Yet Christians differ on this point. Some believe that the christian faith does indeed have a bearing on man's conception of the world and on the course of its culture and civilization. The

---

3. French title: *Le Rôle social des idées,* Paris, Lethielleux, 1936.

extent of this influence is again debated. For some it is quite pronounced, particularly among those who favor the idea of a "Christendom" in the historical sense, whereas others see it as marginal only. But there is also a group who maintain that the proper influence of the christian faith does not consist in "supernaturalizing" the world as such but rather in promoting a sound "secularity." Revelation itself, it is said, inculcates the "secular" status of the world, which man however is to provide with "orientation toward its ultimate, supernatural end." What is being proposed, then, is not a revival of the old Liberalism, for the new "secularity" — the "laical" world of society — is advocated in the name of revelation, somewhat in the manner that M. Carrouges spoke of "an anticlericalism based on faith." [4] In sum, we have divergent views concerning the proper impact of the christian faith on the world. In the pages that follow we shall deal with them in some detail.

Replies and Comments

First, we examine the position and the argument of those who advocate "secularity" [laicïté] in the name of revelation. To be kept in mind throughout the discussion is that when Christians of this group speak of the "world," they mean the totality of culture and civilization, not that aspect which might be considered the "domain" of ecclesial realities. For the world, in this sense, to be "christian" means in their view that it exist and develop according to its own specific laws and under its own autonomy. This is very much the language of the Constitution *Gaudium et Spes*:

> If by autonomy of earthly affairs we mean that created things and societies themselves enjoy their own laws and values which must be gradually deciphered, put to use, and regulated by men, then it is entirely right to demand that autonomy.

---

4. Le Laïcat, mythe et réalité, Paris, Éd. Centurion, 1964.

This is not merely required by modern man, but harmonizes also with the will of the Creator. For by the very circumstance of their having been created, all things are endowed with their own stability, truth, goodness, proper laws and order (no. 36).

The norm of human activity in society and the world is man himself. This, too, echoes the Constitution:

Hence, the norm of human activity is this: that in accord with the divine plan and will, it harmonizes with the genuine good of the human race, and that it allows men as individuals and as members of society to pursue their total vocation and fulfill it (no. 35).

By a theological act of faith and charity the "believer" invests his "worldly" activity with more than worldly meaning, with ultimate meaning, which consists in its ordination to the ultimate end. For a Christian this end is supernatural and, strictly speaking, it is the one and last end of history. The "ultimate reference" denotes and expresses a transcendental relation. Hence, it does not in any way impinge upon the workings and the laws of terrestrial realities. Such is the preliminary posture, the starting point, of the group under discussion, viz., Christians who urge secularity in the name of revelation. Developing their argument, they explain how they conceive of secularity and how they understand the practical influence of the christian faith on man's activity in this world and for this world.

Believers themselves, they contend, ought to be the most ardent supporters of their position. For in professing the general "secularity" of this world they are also professing that the "ultimate" or "absolute" meaning of human existence is not to be found in this world. Hence, they will be witnesses to another "dimension" of life, to an authentic "transcendence," which is attained in the act of theological faith and charity. Failing this transcendent dimension, even believers could succumb to a widespread temptation of the age, namely the temptation to regard the world or the things of the world as inherently endowed with a religious or sacred meaning. And unless care is taken to prevent it, the attribution of sacred meaning and import to the world itself can very easily become a substitute for theological reference to a transcendent God.

These same advocates of "secularity" in the name of revelation anticipate another result of no small consequence. If, that is, the world is stripped of every religious or sacred aspect, no one in his right mind would regard it as an Absolute or search it for the Absolute. Diminished or eliminated would be man's propensity to "deify" this world and to be beholden to it for "idols" or "false gods" and "false absolutes," be they persons (screen stars), possessions (money) or pursuits (pleasure).

In this secular world as here proposed, would there be any practical role at all for christian faith and revelation? Believers, even baptized believers who would say no are, of course, around. For them, the separation between christian faith and activity in the world is absolute. What makes it so is that theological activity and temporal activity are essentially different. Therefore no association is possible. Doubtless, this is an extreme position, one that is reminiscent of an earlier Liberalism. More recently, between the two World Wars, when the Catholic Action movement began to take hold, there was much declaiming against the "shameful divorce" that kept the Church and the world apart. But this was largely on the doctrinal level, a theoretical attack rather than a practical solution. And practical solutions is precisely what the mood of the present generation seems to favor. Empirical answers are apparently "in," metaphysical resolutions "out." Christians of the extreme view we have mentioned could accept, without too much difficulty, a pragmatic arrangement that would allow a Christianity of the pietistic tradition and secular activity that is technologically first-rate go each its own way, a sort of "live and let live" policy, whether for the individual or for their society. This attitude is not necessarily bad, but is it the best? Or the ideal?

On the contrary, revelation could make a more direct contribution to the work which these Christians perform in the
world. It could do this without requiring them to change or
modify their conception of the world's autonomy. Among other
things, revelation provides motivation for conduct, incentive to
action, examples that inspire, deeds to imitate. None of this
encroaches upon the autonomy of the world and human activity
in the world. What revelation can do is to lend support and
encouragement to the "believer" who works in this world. It
says to him: act *like* Christ who gave himself unto death, act
like the apostles who spent themselves for their brethren. And why
act thus? *Because* these men around you are members of Christ's
mystical body, and *in order that* the peace willed by Christ reign
among them and among all men. When revelation plays this role,
the intrinsic structures of human activity are not the least bit
affected; they remain exactly what they were.

In fact, the proponents of complete "secularity" for the world
could make still greater use of revelation, and again without
prejudice to their basic position. They could admit that revelation
proposes, if not a "theology of christian existence in society,"
at least "christian orientations," as in the realm of brotherhood
among men, the promotion of justice and equity, the concern for
peace and harmony and public honesty, etc. Moreover, to all
practical intents and purposes these "revealed and christian"
orientations would coincide with what could be known and
proposed by any man of right disposition, guided, in other words,
by his essentially rational instincts. Revelation would in some
sense *duplicate* the basic orientations of reason.

To repeat we are speaking of fundamental orientations, not
of technical determinations, in which revelation as such has no
jurisdictional competence, hence no specific light of its own to
offer. Revelation does not spell out the dollars-and-cents equivalent of a minimum wage. Also, in regard to reason and revelation
coinciding, the coincidence in question is of the practical order,
in the actual exercise of human affairs. In this order, the guidance

or determination which the "believer's" action receives does not differ from what is available to a properly disposed man exercising his rational faculties. If rice is to be shipped to India, it matters not who is at the helm, a "believer" or a "rationalist." What it takes to move and keep the ship on course is the same, and if it is forthcoming the transport will be on its way.

Another group of Christians, more numerous than the preceding, hold that christian faith and revelation give certain "specific" indications as to the role of society and the Christian's action in society. In consequence of these indications the role and the action in question also become "specific." But "specific" does not mean "completely different" but rather lending a new "touch" or "turn" to certain aspects of an activity that remains essentially as it was. And the same holds true for what comes out of such activity, its results and effects, which will not differ materially from what they would have been without "specific" influence from revelation.

Yet, while admitting the principle of "specific" indications, this group does not altogether agree as to its practical application. As a matter of fact, differences appear both in the theorization and implementation of the principle, and sometimes they are considerable. At one end we find the ideal of a "Christendom" as fostered by medieval Curialists of the Augustinian tradition, at the other those who are only for putting greater emphasis on the christian orientations noted above, especially in certain areas of society. Between these extremes, differences of position run the gamut. However, on the fundamental idea all members of the group are agreed, namely that the existence and progress of the world — culture and civilization — demands, indeed that man's activity in the world fully respect its specific and proper laws, but also and even more, that it respect the indications furnished by christian faith and revelation. To some these indications are quite stringent and compelling, to others much less so.

In general, what is involved here is the "social demands"

of the gospel message. Does the gospel impose specific obliga-
tions toward society? Or, what are the grounds for its "social
demands"? The key to the answer lies in the dignity of the human
person, which, especially in its christian ennoblement, is truly
incomparable. According to the New Testament, all who are
justified partake of God's life. They are "brothers" of Christ.
They are "spiritual," having received the Spirit. Since this is
true of all, it would be as though sinning against one's nature
to deny the qualities of the "human person" to the "family community" or the "work community." In other words, if it is
possible to speak of an "anthropology" inspired by christian
revelation, it is also admissible to form a conception of community
or society, a sociology therefore, of the same inspiration. To
illustrate, when a believer leaves his christian cultural milieu
and visits for the first time a Moslem or Hindu cultural milieu,
does he not get the feeling of being "in another world"? Doubtless,
the same feeling may arise in moving from one christian environment to another. But that proves the point, for we attribute this
difference of cultural climate to — what? To a different conception
of Christianity itself!

We said a moment ago that the Christian receives the Spirit.
It might be helpful, then, to mention what christian revelation
teaches concerning the work of the Spirit in man, in the world
and in the universe. To take but one aspect, we could consider
what is conveyed in the New Testament doctrine of the "fruits
of the Spirit." Briefly, it denotes a "manifestation" of the Spirit,
which is to say a supernatural outpouring of the life of the
Spirit that floods the soul, an interior manifestation but with
visible repercussion, viz., *visible fruitbearing* round about the
Christian and in the community at large.

These "fruits" are numerous, and St. Paul has several lists
(Rom. 14:17; Gal. 5:22; Eph. 4:2-5, 32; 5:2, 9; Col. 3:12-15).
Putting them together, they are: good will, kindness, friendliness,
moderation, gentleness, longsuffering, patience, faithfulness, peace,
modesty, sincerity, joyfulness. All of these qualities are to be

understood as "manifestation," scil. of the Spirit. "In Sacred
Scripture the etymological notion of fruit has more the meaning
of *product* or result than fruition and enjoyment." [5] However,
if there is to be fruit, there must first be abundant interior fructification of the theological life. But also necessary, in fact more
formally and principally contemplated is the visible fructification,
the impingement or impact upon the social milieu. Hence, manifestation of the Spirit betokens both "a divine epiphany in the
christian community" and its repercussion in the community, viz.,
"love of fellow man [*philanthropie*] that is clearly inspired by
divine charity." Here as always, authentic Christianity reveals
itself in super-abundant interior life that overflows and brings
forth fruit in the outer world.

It is rather certain, then, that the christian message does have
a practical bearing on the social order. But we hasten to add —
a point we have made before — that its role is not of a technical
or "scientific" nature. What the message intends is basic directions
for the world, not technical solutions for its problems. Technical
elaboration and solution comprises all the work of theoretical
analysis and assessment, the creation of programs, their practical
refinement and implementation. This is man's work, his proper
field of responsibility. Basic directions means to give emphasis,
to show insistence, to lend support and encouragement, to
show approval and provide orientation. This is the area that pertains to the believer, not (e.g.) as artisan or craftsman but *so
far as* his activity is motivated and guided by the "specific" light
of revelation.[6] The faithful, in the words of *Gaudium et Spes,*
should "not imagine that [their] pastors are always such experts,
that to every problem which arises, however complicated, they
can readily give him a concrete solution" (no. 43). What is
more, "such is not their mission" (*ibid.*). This, then, is an

---

5. M. Ledrus, "Fruits du Saint-Esprit," *La Vie spirituelle,* 1947, p. 717.
6. "Specific," because in this area revelation also, and most of all, provides
"common" orientations, i.e., "similar" to those founded on human
reason.

initial restriction, one of great importance, that should govern all attempts to determine the requirements or "demands of the gospel message" so far as it is concerned with the societal life of man.

It is imperative to have a clear understanding of the distinction between basic direction on the one hand and technical elaboration. There are Christians who seem to think that revelation is to provide the *general principles* and human science the *technical precisions*. But that is not the case. In matters of culture and civilization it is man that thinks and theorizes, assembles and marshals data, analyzes, elaborates and refines whatever the problem calls for. Faith, for its part, inspires certain choices, stresses certain qualities and values, disesteeming others, etc. Human efforts towards settling human problems do not always meet with success or complete agreement. The requirements or demands of revelation concerning culture and civilization are even more difficult to determine. Again to the point is *Gaudium et Spes*: "Often enough the christian view of things will itself suggest some specific solution in certain circumstances. Yet it happens rather frequently, and legitimately so, that with equal sincerity some of the faithful will disagree with others on a given matter" (no. 43). In any event, we should not depend on revelation for more than it offers, "general" directions and orientations, certainly most valuable and desirable and fruitful, but nevertheless always "general," such as: brotherhood, justice, equity, peace and harmony, truthfulness, goodness, etc. As for establishing certain *"specifically christian"* positions in dealing with the social order, and maintaining that they are demanded by the gospel message, we would only say that such attempts call for mature deliberation, a mentality that knows how to be prudent and moderate and, most of all, never forgets the limitations within which it must make its point.

Christians who profess "secularity" offer the following in reply to the exponents of "specificity," of which we have been speaking. Assuming (they argue) that the influence of revelation does exist and that it has a kind of "specificity," would it not be better in dealing with the present world to disregard it, at least for the time being, and to act as though it did not exist? Why? Because (they contend) this influence, as far as its "specific" character is concerned, is so tenuous and nebulous, so little discernible that many question its existence. And speaking of the practical level, the area of concrete social action, is there really *that* much difference between the demands of "christian" brotherhood and "human" brotherhood, or between those of "christian" justice and "human" justice? Being so little perceptible, the practical effect of the allegedly "specific" demand of revelation would be correspondingly small, in fact minimal if not altogether illusory. Besides, by insisting on the specific factor contained or possibly contained in the revealed influence, we invite the temptation to neglect the common ground of all men, Christian or not. This is a sizable portion, for it covers practically the whole area of justice and brotherhood about which men must be concerned today. Add to this the undeniable circumstance that the human problems which the present world faces are so vast and complex that to solve them effectively all men, irrespective of their beliefs, must join in the effort.

These considerations deserve to be taken into account. But some theologians would say, and rightly so, that the interpretation of human nature which is at least implied in the case of "secularity" is already influenced by the christian revelation. It is a conception which, ideally speaking, man's reason can arrive at but which in practice and without the help of God's word and revelation, the generality of men do not achieve, or only with great difficulty and no small admixture of error (Denz. 1786). Not surprisingly perhaps, the other side sees the matter differently. Since their view of man *is* discoverable by human reason, that is but another reason not to insist on what is "specific" to the Christian.

A final point, which is still part of the "secularity" argument, gets back to the enormity of the problems confronting all men today and the necessity of concerted effort for effective solutions. The contention is that the "specificity" attitude hampers such

effort. In other words, having badly understood and badly interpreted what was thought to be "specific" to revelation, Christians
have more than once been found to accept as a christian ideal
what was in fact a major overstatement of the true demands
of revelation in regard to the world (e.g., the ideal of a "Christendom," the Galileo case, the substitution of "cult" for social
justice). Would it not be better to avoid all that? The question
comes from the "secularity" group.

PART THREE

Agreements and Reservations

To which this writer may be allowed to add this comment, if only to balance the picture. Unquestionably, the christian ideal has suffered abuse. But do they come off exonerated, those who flatly reject the idea of "something more," "something plus" which many are convinced revelation can bring to bear upon the world. They, too, have tolerated injustices, have made mistakes and (quite possibly) committed wrongs one way or other. Humanism "without God" is not necessarily proof against the shortcomings, imperfections and failings that plague the rest of mankind. In sum, "laicity" has not yet won everybody, and "secularity" too has still to prove itself.

In this last section we return to the theologians and theological positions which were introduced in the first part to serve as reference points for our discussion of the contemporary faith-vs-religion movement. In the middle section, just concluded, we reviewed the essential features of a Catholic doctine of faith, touching also on its full development, its forms of expression and its social ramifications and implications. That review leads naturally to the next and final consideration, viz. faith, particularly the Catholic faith, as seen by the aforesaid theologians, with special attention to the visible dimension of faith, its institutional economy and its social or community-related import. Need we say that we have no intention to "refute" these authors? Our only aim is to show why and where, in the light of the middle section, we sometimes take issue with them, as well as to acknowledge their positive contribution, a goodly amount in all, to Christian theological thought.

I

Karl Barth

Religion, in Barth's view, is essentially a human work aimed at self-justification and self-redemption, man's attempt, that is, to save and sanctify himself — by himself alone. Doubtless, every religion faces this danger or temptation. But to make this misguided effort the heart and soul, the very essence and definition of religion is a far different matter, and Barth himself could not have done it except for his particular notion of faith and of the Church. It is a notion, need we add, which Catholic theologians feel obliged to call in question.

Religion

The passage quoted from Barth at the beginning illustrate the antithesis, the opposing factors, on which his thought builds and which reappears again and again in his writings. On the one side is a sovereign and free God, on the other a man or a community — God according sinful man the gift of grace, man on the other hand attempting to secure it by himself, striving to "place the hand" on God and wanting "guarantees," as though he had a "right" to grace. No one would deny that these are two possible approaches to Christianity and that examples can be found for either one. But to present the first as Protestant doctrine and attribute the other, albeit obliquely, to Catholicism would be a more than questionable simplification. Catholics, it should be fairly obvious, would not recognize themselves in this description of "religion." But since it has been possible to attribute this sort of Christianity to them, it may be assumed that some of their attitudes lend themselves to such interpretation.

And if that be so, they ought to stop and listen to what is being said of them.

Every religion admittedly runs the risk of becoming a "great" institution which offers itself to the faithful for the purpose of saving them, or that they might save themselves. In view of the importance of its social activity, this danger is perhaps more real for Catholicism than for most religions. But probably more important in this connection is the Catholic doctrine of "merit," which seems to suggest that Catholics "save" themselves.

No doubt, the inspired writings teach that the Lord will render to each according to his works. Christian revelation speaks of different sanctions for the good and the wicked. St. Paul does not shrink from the term "wages" (I Cor. 3:8, 14). He sees a correlation between wages and the toil of the laborer (I Cor. 3:8). He teaches that suffering borne for God produces an "eternal weight of glory" (II Cor. 4:17) and that injustice will meet with retribution: "who does a wrong will get back the wrong he did" (Col. 3:25). This is strong scriptural support, obviously, but the question is whether it justifies our entire theology of "merit."

Actually, "merit" is not a biblical term, and the idea of merit itself is not always perfectly clear. Primarily it is a legal term, relating to matters of justice. Taking the term in this juridical connotation, our good works, even when considered as the fruit of grace, cannot be called meritorious in the strict sense. If they merit at all, it is in a secondary or accommodated sense, *secundum quid* says St. Thomas.[1] They do not create a relation of strict justice between us and God.

> The just man does not merit in the proper sense. Properly understood the relation of grace to glory is not simply reducible to the legal categories of right or justice. We should rather speak of God producing a correspondence in the soul with a certain order of things, correspondence that is already a real begin-

---

1. *Summa theol.* Ia, IIae, q. 114, a. 1.

ning and a real becoming of heaven, of its gradual ripening, and if a beginning, then also an *ontological requirement of its coming to full term*.[2]

When God deposits the seed of glory in us, he is pursuing his plan of sanctification, for it is his will that we be holy. Having begun this work, he is not one to leave it unfinished. The seed calls for growth and maturation, for perfect fulfillment. Our moral life, in all its forms, is not primarily a "means" of this fulfillment, of gaining heaven, but rather as though a consequence or result of the supernatural life received from God. Better still, the more the Christian grows in the life of grace and in his configuration to Christ, the more he approaches the complete selflessness that was Christ's and the pure liberality of Providence. At the pinnacle of holiness, in the perfection of love, the soul's selflessness is at its highest, bordering on and indeed participating in the utterly gratuitous manner of God's loving.

Barth is preoccupied with the opposition (or what is thought to be opposition) between faith and religion. In developing this theme he pushes to the limit the contrast and tension between the Old Covenant and the New, between Law and Gospel, Flesh and Spirit, Faith and Works. This can be seen in *The Epistle to the Romans* published in 1919,[3] the famous commentary on the Pauline letter. Barth is radical. Not only does he define Christianity as the pure gift of God, but man's response — his acceptance, his faith — is likewise pure grace, the work of God alone: God responding to himself in man. On this point H. Kraemer, though an advocate of "dialectical"[4] theology, raises

---

2. L. Malevez, "Histoire et Réalités dernières," *Ephem. Théol. Lovan.* 19 (1942), p. 71.
3. *The Epistle to the Romans,* trans. from 6th edition by Edwyn C. Hoskyns (London, Oxford University Press, 1933; 6th impression, 1963).
4. A theology is said to be "dialectical" if it attempts to express the "tension that necessarily pervades every theological formulation," from the fact that there is question of God and of man, of grace and of

some serious doubts, even from the Calvinist point of view. "Calvin," he writes, "let it be understood that despite their weaknesses and faults, there is in religions a kind of vague conversation with God the Father of Jesus Christ.... The monolithic manner in which Barth states the problem leaves no possibility of bringing out the positive significance in the greatness of human religions, which he nevertheless acknowledges, nor the negative significance of demoniacal aberrations, which in spite of everything are yet in relation with God.... The Bible, for all its uncompromising attitude, is much too laden with bold, provocative wisdom to stay capsuled in theological categories."[5]

Faith

How faith stands to religion or the Church depends, obviously, how one understands them, especially the act of faith. In posing the question Barth assumes an interpretation of man's part in this act that Catholics cannot accept without reservation. Nor can they accept without reservation his understanding of the means of sanctification instituted by Christ.

The act of faith is an act of grace, through and through. But it is also a "human" act, free and conscious. God inspires this act from beginning to end in all its aspects. God's doing, however, does not necessarily result in the human reality of this act being nullified, nor in its being "mine" only so far as it is not really an act of faith. Barth, according to H. Bouillard, seems to create a rift within the act of faith itself by putting the act, which is from man, on one side and faith, which is solely from God, on the other. And he maintains the same partition as regards justification. There is no denying, of course, that it

---

sin, of the "already-there" and the "not-yet." Hence, the only way, apparently, to keep theological speculation true to reality is to proceed by way of "yes" and "no," by interpretations which, though "unveilings" in one respect, are but new "veilings" in another — in short, by way of paradox.

5. H. Kraemer, *La Foi chrétienne et les Religions non chrétiennes*, p. 80 (Neuchâtel, Delachaux et Niestlé, 1956).

is God who produces the faith in us. But what he produces is precisely our act. In fact, this is what characterizes God's creation in general, viz., that creatures also are agents in the true sense of the word. In his concern that all human cooperation with the divine action be excluded Barth, while affirming in one breath the autonomous role of the believing subject, nevertheless seems to reduce it to the vanishing point in the next.

> As we have seen, if man in the act of believing has the status of subject, it is only provisionally, i.e., so far as he functions as predicate of the subject God. If we had to take this strictly, we should be faced with a form of pantheism. At the very least, Barth's phrasing of it would justify the term "panentheism," which is E. Prsywara's characterization of his thought. We would gladly regard this as a *lapsus* on Barth's part, that he really did not mean what he said, if he had not said the same thing elsewhere, namely that the relation of the believer to the Word of God is not a relation of subject to object but of predicate to subject; in other words, that the reality of man precisely as reality that encounters the Word of God does not exist in itself and for itself but only as given with and in (*mitgesetzt in*) this same Word. As the immediate context makes clear, it is again a case of excluding all cooperation with the divine work. It seems to us that in parting, as we have shown, from St. Paul's doctrine Barth was led in spite of himself to compromise the autonomous reality of the believing subject.[6]

But Barth notwithstanding, it is of the utmost importance to maintain both in theory and practice, the two dimensions or aspects of the act of faith, difficult though it be to formulate and, even more, to live them properly. There is the dimension of the free choice, not in diminished form but in its full reality. This is a conscious and decisive act. Every man is the subject of this

6. H. Bouillard, *Karl Barth* (Paris, Aubier, 1957), vol. III, pp. 24-25.

act and every man's destiny is fixed by it. There is also the divine dimension, the radical disproportion between man's act and the salvific work that is a gift of God, gift of communion with him, with his life and knowledge, gift of himself that he alone can bestow. These two aspects of one and the same act of faith do not constitute a "collaboration" of two equal agents, having the same nature and the same attributes. That is not how the Bible understands this unparalleled and paradoxical yet very real joint action, this "synergia" (I Cor. 3:9). Nor do these two aspects of the one act of faith imply some kind of "reciprocity," as though God and man had reciprocal claim on each other, or reciprocal rights. That, too, is not how the Bible understands it, this event born solely of the goodness of God and sealed in a covenant, the New Covenant, the *kainè diathèkè* (I Cor. 11:25).

The Church

In Barth's view the Church is exclusively a Church of the Word of God. It is founded solely on the Word of God.[7] It is the community of all believers among whom the pure gospel is preached and the holy sacraments are administered conformably to the gospel (Augsburg Confession). There, and only there, does the Church exist, i.e., in the preaching of the gospel and the administration of sacraments. This is not to say that Barth denies the visible side of the Church, which as a matter of fact he wanted to be of greater significance, not less. For though he professes that it is God alone who enables man to receive his revelation, he also declares that God does so in a determined place, which is the place of the Church.[8] Practically speaking,

---

7. For Barth's ecclesiology see, e.g., J. Hamer, *Karl Barth*, pp. 139-186 (for translation, etc., see Part III, chap. 1, note 13); Ch. Journet, *L'Église du Verbe incarné*, II, 1129-1171 (Désclee De Brouwer); H. Fries, *Kirche als Ereignis*, pp. 68-118 (Düsseldorf, 1958).

8. "God Himself and God alone turns man into a recipient of His revelation — but He does so in a definite area, and this area, if we may now combine the Old Testament and the New Testament, is the area

what characterizes the visible Church is genuine acceptance of
the inspired writings as decisive norm. This is its distinctive mark.

The visible Church, to put it another way, is it nothing more
than "the ecclesiastical machinery irradiated by the lightning of
the gospel"? [9] And the preaching of the authorized minister, our
(human) word, with its weakness and folly, is it only "an earthen
vessel which lodges the riches of the word of God." [10] In Barth's
ecclesiology the Church, while having the assurance of divine
indefectibility, appears nevertheless in intermittent form: it *exists*
in the midst of the visible structure *when* the event of the Word
occurs. "The essence of the Church is the event by which sacred
Scripture in its function as prophetic and apostolic witness of
Jesus Christ produces the demonstration of the Spirit and of
power, and thereby the proof of its intrinsic truth." [11] "If the
Church believes it can exist apart from the event of the Holy
Spirit, it has only the semblance of the Church and its unity
is necessarily destroyed." [12]

In Catholic ecclesiology the visible accouterment of the Church
has greater theological significance. It is an element of the
New Covenant concluded between God and man through the
mediation of our Lord Jesus Christ. Of his own sovereign will
and his own sovereign authority the Lord instructed us to baptize,
and to celebrate the Last Supper, adding (in the first instance)
"He who is baptized will be saved" and (elsewhere) "Who hears
you, hears me." As understood by Catholics, New Testament revelation indicates that the bond between the absolutely gratuitous
grace of God and the rites or ceremonies of the Church is more
intimate and more vital than suggested by Barth.

of the Church" (*Church Dogmatics,* I, 2, 210; for translation, etc., see
Part III, chap. 1, note 6).

9. Ch. Journet, *L'Église du Verbe incarné,* II, 1140.
10. Karl Barth, *Parole de Dieu et parole humaine,* p. 221 (Paris, Ed. Je-
sers, 1933).
11. Karl Barth, "La Nature et la Forme de l'Église," *Cahiers protestants*
(Lausanne, March 1948), p. 77.
12. *Ibid.,* p. 80.

According to J. Hamer, O.P., Barth's position has to be regarded as "theological occasionalism." For, the Church and the Bible itself are not primarily a sign or instrument but rather a *place,* the normal place for the sudden and mysterious event of the Word of God, hence in some way an *occasion* for this event to overtake the sinner and traverse the soul as though swept by lightning. Catholic theologians cannot see where this conception reflects biblical teaching. And that is why they are of the opinion that the Word of God is not the sole source of Barth's thought.

Apropos of God's judgment on religions Barth has said that "everything is in order because we are in the presence of the order established by God." [13] So far as this states a principle, we can only agree with him. But it may be questioned whether his representation of the order established by God is truly adequate. And whether the alternative he offers to purely human religion on the one hand, and revelation without religion on the other, accords with the revealed Word. As yet, this has not been demonstrated to everyone's satisfaction. Religion, taken on its merits alone, he regards as "sham," "deceit," "injustice," "horror." It becomes just and holy when impregnated by revelation. However, his understanding of the relationship between religion and revelation appears to be specifically Protestant rather than essentially or universally christian. This is not to deny, for it cannot be denied, that Barth deserves acclaim for his lifelong, heroic defense of a fundamental aspect of christian life that is sometimes imperiled both among Protestants and Catholics. But because his success in this regard is unquestionable, it must not be thought that he is always right and never to be questioned.

---

13. *Church Dogmatics,* I, 2, 354.

II

Dietrich Bonhoeffer

New insights into his life appeared in a French study of Dietrich Bonhoeffer by René Marlé.[1] Undoubtedly, those who had known of this Lutheran pastor only from certain English works written by exponents of de-sacralization were in for some surprises. In any case, and in keeping with the general plan of our study, we have now to take up again certain aspects of Bonhoeffer's thought.

An Adult World

The first point Bonhoeffer makes is this: man has come of age. He is now in his maturity, an adult. The implications of this are far-reaching indeed. For,

> our coming of age leads us to a true recognition of our situation before God. God would have us know that we must live as men who manage our lives without him .... The God who lets us live in the world without the working hypothesis of God is the God before whom we stand continually. Before God and with God we live without God.[2]

The world, then, has come of age. It would be captious to point out that the great majority of mankind have not yet come

---

1. Casterman, 1967.
2. *Letters and Papers from Prison*, p. 196 (for translation, etc., see Part I, chap. 2, note 2). Throughout this chapter, citations from this work are identified in the text proper, the parenthesized pagination referring in each instance to it.

that far, that we still have a long way to go stamping out mere illiteracy. The fact is that no one really wants to remain at that subcultural level, and men generally are trying to make the benefits of culture and civilization available to all people. The Constitution *Gaudium et Spes,* a pastoral document, makes a strong plea for the general advancement of mankind, for cultural and economic improvement wherever it is lagging. A measure of its vision is that some critics feel it may have gone too far too fast, overestimating the actual state of human development, because it seems to speak as though all the world had already come of age. One thing is certain. We should all rejoice if all Catholics, at least, were in fact "adult," and accepted the responsibilities of adulthood.

In Bonhoeffer's lexicon, to come of age means especially to become "autonomous." From the beginning man has had to cope with problems: of life, health, weather, housing, world conditions, etc. When he was unable to meet them, he sought help in a *deus ex machina* that served as "stop-gap" or remedy to his ignorance and helplessness. As time went on, however, he grew in ability to help himself. In fact, man has now

> learnt to deal with himself in all questions of importance without recourse to the "working hypothesis" called "God." In questions of science, art, and ethics this has become an understood thing at which one now hardly dares to tilt. But for the last hundred years or so it has also become increasingly true of religious questions; it is becoming evident that everything gets along without "God" — and, in fact, just as well as before (p. 178).

Man, in short, has progressed from the cave man he once was. But we need not go back that far. The Hebrew of old believed that God made the rain, sent the hail, quelled the storm. The Catholic of today does not believe this — precisely as the Hebrew did. The question is not whether we should expect scientific explanations from the Bible. We know we shouldn't. It is rather that what the Hebrews attributed directly to God we, quite properly, attribute to meteorological conditions.[3] For created causes of which he was ignorant ancient man substituted the uncreated Cause. This is a recognized fact, and occurs in all religions of the past, if not of the present. Says *Gaudium et Spes,* "Many benefits once looked for, especially from heavenly powers, man has now enterprisingly procured for himself" (no. 33).

The Constitution takes cognizance of this development and endorses it wholeheartedly. It affirms at considerable length the worth and value of earthly realities and underscores their autonomy.[4]

If by the autonomy of earthly affairs we mean that created things and societies themselves enjoy their own laws and values which must be gradually deciphered, put to use, and regulated by man, then it is entirely right to demand that autonomy. This is not merely required by modern man, but harmonizes also with the will of the Creator. For by the very circumstance of their having been created, all things are endowed with their own stability, truth, goodness, proper laws and order. Man must respect these as he isolates them by the appropriate methods of the individual sciences or arts (no. 36).

Before saying this the Constitution had expressed itself on human activity, in part as follows:

Throughout the course of the centuries, men have labored to better the circumstances of their lives through a monumental amount of individual and collective effort. To believers, this point is settled: considered in itself, this human

3. As regards the way Israel envisioned Divine Providence, see J. Bonsirven, *Le Judaïsme palestinien,* vol. 1, pp. 175-182 (Paris, Beauchesne, 1934).
4. *Gaudium et Spes,* nos. 34, 36, 39.

activity accords with God's will. For man, created to God's image, received a mandate to subject to himself the earth and all it contains, and to govern the world with justice and holiness; a mandate to relate himself and the totality of things to Him Who was to be acknowledged as the Lord and Creator (no. 34).

The Constitution does not say that we should attribute the phenomena of nature directly to God, by-passing created causes, but should acknowledge him as Creator and relate all things to him as ultimate cause. God cannot be turned into a *deus ex machina* or "stop-gap" God. If a Christian is under that illusion, he has simply to get rid of it — someone or something must make him see where he is wrong. God, that is, is not merely someone who can come to our assistance when we have reached the limits of our efforts and still not solved our problems. And certainly this need of him at the "limits" is no argument for his existence. For that, more basic, more metaphysical reasoning is needed, which in outline is as follows:

> The metaphysical reasoning that ends by affirming God's existence involves two steps. The first establishes the existence of an *absolute* or unconditioned *reality*. The second demonstrates that this absolute reality must be sought *outside finite beings,* which is to say that it transcends the finite, or is infinite.[5]

What the Constitution *Gaudium et Spes* clearly frowns upon is the "let God do it" attitude even where man could or should do it. It is a "supernaturalist" attitude in the sense that it gives hardly any practical recognition to the reality of "second causes." Yet we find considerable evidence of this tendency in the Bible, in the Fathers, in Christian liturgy and catechesis and also in christian spirituality. For example, it is God who

---

5. F. van Steenberghen, *Dieu caché,* p. 197 (Louvain, 1961).

covers the heavens with clouds,
prepares rain for the earth,
makes grass grow upon the hills,
and herbs for the service of men (Ps. 146:8).

But the tendency still exists, and it constitutes an obstacle
to sound progress, to the efforts that would bring it about. Indeed, it has been argued that the kind of prayer it inspires makes
for a "real social problem [especially] in underdeveloped countries." [6]

This brings up the question of "religions," a veritable thorn
in the flesh of Bonhoeffer. What he found most obnoxious —
"nauseous" would really be the term — was that religions, in
his appraisal, deliberately sought to contain man in his weaknesses and limitations, the better to persuade him that only religion (or only God) could provide the answers he seeks and the
help he needs. The God of religion, it seemed to him, was only
a God of solution to "insoluble problems" and "human limitations,"
problems such as the fear of death (pp. 123, 155), the anguish
of sin (p. 155), the mystery of suffering (p. 175), etc. It is on
these "ultimate questions" that religion thrives and which it
exploits when "there has been surrender [scil. by religion] on
all secular problems" (p. 178). What it all comes to is an odious
campaign of "religious exploitation" (p. 154) in which, of all
things, religion is aided and abetted by existential philosophy
and the professional psychotherapist. Typical of his general
protest is the following:

I should like to speak of God not on the boundaries but
at the center, not in weaknesses but in strength; and therefore not in death and guilt but in man's life and goodness.
As to the boundaries, it seems to me better to be silent and

6. See Cl. Souffrant, "Des prières qui font obstacle à la libération des
masses sous-développees," *Parole et Mission,* 9 (no. 35, 1966), pp.
592-611.

leave the insoluble unsolved. Belief in the resurrection is *not* the "solution" of the problem of death. God's "beyond" is not the beyond of our cognitive faculties (p. 155).

Here again, it must be admitted, Bonhoeffer is saying much that makes sense. For, it is true that God is not just a crutch to reach for when we are in distress, a kind of cure-all to our ills and handicaps, be they physical, moral or intellectual. God is as much the God of life as of death, of health as of sickness, of the gifted as of the less endowed. And the "immortality of the soul" that philosophers discuss is not the equivalent of "glorious resurrection," such as will be wrought through the Spirit of the Lord. There may be Christians whom the shoe fits, who live and think as Bonhoeffer represents them. If so, they have a badly needed work of aggiornamento to perform in themselves.

But all is not plus for Bonhoeffer, either. To identify religions with ventures that "exploit" the limit-situations of man, his inescapable circumscriptions, this is very much like generalizing from a particular case. If some "pious" souls may be charged with the aberrations described by Bonhoeffer, and if all religions are threatened by the same aberrations, and even if all religions do sometimes yield to them, are we therefore justified to define religion by its abuses, to identify the deformity with the normality? Or, if the search and scientific study of God starts from finite being — what else could it start from? — and then arrives at absolute Being, is that "blackmail"? And if Christ chose the Cross, and the Resurrection, is it "exploitation" to inculcate the significance and the value of suffering in the christian scheme of things? And finally, religionless Christianity, will it be proof against hazard and temptation?

Religionless Christianity

In reading Bonhoeffer the question that keeps cropping up is what exactly does he mean by "nonreligious" or "religionless" Christianity. His remarks on the subject are sporadic rather than sustained, so that it is difficult to get a complete or sharply-defined picture. Nevertheless, the basic development comes through, and follows a consistent pattern. In substance, it is this. God has been proposed as the solution to an infant world (pp. 178, 179). But man is now an adult. He has outgrown the solution — God. This God, in fact, is losing ground with each passing day, and soon the Church will have to face the prospect of a pastoral ministry addressed to an "irreligious" world. But the purpose of the ministry will not be to bring men back to "religion" but rather to offer them a nonreligious Christianity, a gospel interpreted in a "nonreligious" and "secular" sense (pp. 155, 157), and conveyed in a "new language, perhaps quite nonreligious" (p. 172).

The outpouring of terms like "irreligious," "nonreligious," "without religion," or "religionless" is, to say the least, perplexing. And the perplexity only increases when it is remembered that during this period Bonhoeffer was also writing at length and approvingly of baptism, that he wished to take communion, and that he persevered in prayer — a paradox indeed, that a man of such christian loyalties should at the same time be so vehemently opposed to (in his phrase) "christian religion." And so the question: what exactly does he have in mind? A certain *type* of Christianity, or every form of christian *religion,* absolutely and without exception?

Bonhoeffer's quarrel, apparently, is with a certain type of Christianity. He refers specifically to a certain "pietism," which he rejects. As described by him, in the broadest of terms, most Christians would also reject it, for they are well aware that Christ drew a far different picture of his Father and his Church — different, that is, from what Bonhoeffer saw in "pietism." As a matter of fact, however, his opposition does not stop there. On the contrary, he voices a sort of refusal of all christian "religion," or better perhaps, a foreboding that we are moving into a new era in which the "Church's form will have changed" (p. 172) and the Word of God will be proclaimed "in a new language, perhaps quite nonreligious" (p. 172).

Bonhoeffer does not make this suggestion lightly. He thinks it important enough to point out where it places him in relation to Karl Barth and Rudolph Bultmann. This would seem to indicate that he wants theology to take a hand in bringing about the change of direction for the pastoral ministry. Barth, he believes, performed a great service in one respect but is disappointing in another.

> Barth was the first theologian to begin the criticism of religion, and that remains his really great merit; but he puts in its place a positivist doctrine of revelation which says, in effect, "like it or lump it"; virgin birth, Trinity, or anything else; each is an equally significant and necessary part of the whole, which must simply be swallowed as a whole or not at all. That is not biblical (pp. 156-157).

And so, concludes Bonhoeffer — perhaps a little prematurely —what Barth proposes is really nothing more than a "restoration" (p. 153). Bultmann's work, he felt, was more effective, especially his efforts in regard to "de-mythologization."

> My view of it today would be, not that he went "too far," as most people thought, but that he did not go far enough. It is not only the "mythological" concepts, such as miracle, ascension, and so on (which are not in principle separable from the concepts of God, faith, etc.), but "religious" concepts generally, which are problematic. You cannot, as Bultmann supposes, separate God and miracle, but you must be able to interpret and proclaim *both* in a "non-religious" sense (p. 156).

What does it mean to "interpret in a non-religious sense"? Bultmann does not answer this question, or rather — and this is not without significance — he answers by asking, and answering, its opposite, "what does it mean to interpret in a *religious* sense"? "I think," he says, "it means to speak on the one hand metaphysically, and on the other hand individualistically. Neither of these is relevant to the Bible message or to the man of today" (p. 156). From the standpoint of the Bible, "righteousness and the Kingdom of God on earth [are] the focus of everything" (p. 156). Our concern is not to be with "the beyond . . . but with this world as created and preserved, subjected to laws, reconciled, and restored" (p. 156). According to the gospel, what is above this world is intended to exist *for* this world, but (he goes on to explain) "I mean that, not in the anthropocentric sense of liberal, mystic pietistic, ethical theology, but in the biblical sense of the creation and of the incarnation, crucifixion, and resurrection of Jesus Christ" (p. 156). In other words, to be *for* the world in the manner of Christ is a far different thing from "leaving clear a space for religion in the world or against the world" (p. 180).

Up to a point we could agree with Bonhoeffer. If the focus of the christian faith is "God the Savior" or "Jesus Christ the Savior," then the Church he instituted will also be his "salvific" instrument, which is to say it will be *for* the world. However, as far as the Church is concerned it is possible to emphasize either its existence (seeing that an institution is established and maintained) or its *purpose,* the reason for its existence (because mankind is called to become a sanctified community in Christ). Some are preoccupied with the existence of the Church, confident that the sanctification or the judgment of the world will necessarily follow. Others are more interested in the sanctification or the judgment, but *with* the ecclesiastical institution. When they say *with* it is not always clear if they mean "thanks to" or merely "concomitant with," which practically speaking is really equivalent to "without" (benefit of) the ecclesiastical institution. The first leave a place for the Church in the world, either for or against the world. The second live in the world and wish themselves to be signs of grace or of divine judgment. For a Catholic it is not a question of alternatives: *existence* or *purpose.* In the past, it is true, we have strongly emphasized the benefits of the Church's existence, believing that the results would automatically follow and its purpose be achieved. Perhaps we ought to reverse the emphasis, stressing first the purpose, the reason for the Church, viz., to produce a universal community sanctified in Christ, or a world renewed in Christ.

Bonhoeffer's call for existence *for* another is couched in his best manner, direct and incisive. "The Church is the Church only when it exists for another" (p. 211). Living for Jesus, i.e., "being there" entirely for others, this is your "experience of transcendence" (p. 209).

> Our relation to God is not a "religious" relationship to the highest, most powerful, and best Being imaginable — that is not authentic transcendence — but our relation to God is a new life in "existence for others," through participation in the being of Jesus (p. 210).

That God is the "best Being imaginable," or more precisely, is above anything we can imagine no Christian doubts. God is not, strictly speaking, an "extension" (p. 209) of what is best in this world. We might also grant that every relationship or communication with the transcendent takes place through a human mediation, the perfect expression of which is in the one mediator Jesus Christ. It is in him and with him that we come to the Father, through him and with him that we meet our fellow men. Of course, in putting it this way we need to keep in mind certain qualifications and distinctions, especially the most radical distinction of all, the one between the Creator and the creature.

Once it has been decided that the *purpose* of the Church should be the first concern, that before all else we should strive to make the world a community of brotherhood in which peace and justice and goodness reign, a community rich in every fruit of the Spirit, a prelude of the Kingdom of God to come — once this is accepted, the next step is the question of language, how to go about the "secular interpretation of biblical concepts" (p. 193). "I am thinking," says Bonhoeffer, "how we can reinterpret in a 'worldly' sense — in the sense of the Old Testament and of John 1:14 — the concepts of repentance, faith, justification, rebirth, and sanctification" (p. 156). The task will be formidable because "reconciliation and redemption, regeneration and the Holy Ghost, love of enemies, cross and resurrection, life in Christ and christian discipleship — all these things are so difficult and so remote that we hardly venture any more to speak of them" (p. 172). Nevertheless, these things await and must have this "new language," which "will shock people and yet overcome them by its power; it will be the language of a new righteousness and truth, proclaiming God's peace with men and the coming of his kingdom" (p. 172).

If these utterances leave the reader confused or bewildered, it could be because Bonhoeffer's position, as he himself informs us, was still "very much in the early stages" (pp. 177-178) of development. The difficulty, however, seems to be more than a matter of insufficient development. In other words, we may readily admit that themes like the christian love of enemies or christian discipleship have constantly to be explored and made more relevant to the times, but is it really true that they are so "remote" to our age that "we hardly venture any more to speak of them"? And even an adult world, a world come of age, would it have a better understanding of Christianity if we spoke to it of "the man for others, ... the Crucified" (p. 210), or of the "God of the Bible, who wins power and space in the world by his weakness"? Yet of such specimens, presumably, will the language of *secular interpretation* be fashioned (p. 197).

This is not to deny that Bonhoeffer did come to grips with certain needs and demands of contemporary Christianity. It is to be hoped, however, that theological dialogue can provide some much-needed clarification of his thought. Meanwhile, what follows is an attempt to illustrate certain attitudes among Christians which came under Bonhoeffer's criticism.

To designate the work to be accomplished in the world, or amid its culture and civilization, we use theological and biblical terms, which is to say terms that are "religious" or "sacred": e.g., redemption, sanctification, justification, salvation. These terms, however, connote activity that is performed in a domain which, in reality, is not "sacred" but "profane," as these words are used today. So, for example, we have it from *Lumen Gentium* (no. 34) that in actuality the "priesthood of the faithful" and the "spiritual worship" of baptized persons are to be identified with their conjugal and family life, with their leisure and occupation, their prayers and their sufferings and hardships, provided all these things are done or borne in the Spirit. Consequently, we perform an act of this priesthood and this worship whenever we perform an act of conjugal or family life, an act of work or leisure, as well as whenever an act of prayer. The Christian who looks upon his "common priesthood" as something additional to, or *alongside* of his family life, his occupation, his leisure, etc., something he exercises only when he prays, such a Christian has not grasped its true meaning. And the practical consequences of his mistaken notion may be far-reaching, since it could be a determining factor in the interpretation of a Christian "ideal" and how to live it. Perhaps at fault is the word "priesthood" itself, which seems easily misunderstood. The point we wish to make is that Bonhoeffer's reaction, not necessarily to this but to situations of this kind, is both understandable and acceptable. And *Lumen Gentium* supports him.

Another aspect of christian life where better understanding may be needed concerns love of neighbor. Christian spirituality has always taught the primacy of theological charity and of the twofold commandment of love of God and neighbor. St. John asks, "How can he who does not love his brother, whom he sees, love God, whom he does not see?" (I, 4:20). Love of neighbor is made pure and perfect when it is exercised according to Christ's teaching, which is to say when it is truly "christian." That is why Christians are told "to love their neighbor in God and God in their neighbor." Although theological, or rather because it is theological, love of neighbor must be realistic or in keeping with the exigencies and actualities of the situation. But here again misguided efforts and attitudes are possible.

To be theological, love of neighbor must have its primary source in the divine *agápe,* in God's own love. Through grace we live and abide in God's love. The Spirit by his gift, makes us participants of this love which, in a way, is diffused in and through our deed of love toward neighbor. Moreover, under the impulse of this love we see our neighbor and ourselves in the same light, the light that is born of God's presence in us and enables us to discern the reality of the neighbor in its composition with the mystery of God's people.

But if love is to unite me with my neighbor, I — whether in word, deed or bearing — I must take him as he is, both a bodily and spiritual being, and I must be concerned with his welfare rather than my own. Every expression of love toward him requires me to abide by certain rules or principles, depending on the realities of the situation. Whether I am caring for the sick, teaching the alphabet, preparing a lunch, rendering technical assistance, counseling married couples, supervising recreation, arranging vacations, or anything else — all must be done according to all the "rules of the art," i.e., according to the specific requirements of the task I am performing.

Unfortunately, love of neighbor can be improperly understood, especially in regard to its practical implications. For though love is of the essence of the theological life, this life itself can be abused. The sick must have care, but it should be good care and the right kind. Technical assistance should be competent. Recreation should be truly recreative. But these conditions are not automatically assured just because a person is making a conscientious effort to live theologically. If anyone is under this illusion, he is not serving the cause of the theological life, in fact he is giving it a bad name. In their mistaken notion of theological living such individuals seem to think that because they are cultivating the "interior life," they are more or less excused from the "rules of the art," i.e., from acquiring the skills and observing the rules and regulations pertaining specifically to the services they are rendering. The public consequences for the theological life are damaging. For, instead of bearing witness for it, they are (in effect) doing the opposite, scandalously testifying against it.

Given attitudes of this kind, we can appreciate the clamor for "secularization" of theological notions. Better, it is said, to be under the competent care of an atheist doctor than the incompetent care of a saint. This is a pointed illustration of what we are trying to get across. Like most illustrations of this kind, however, it suffers from the weakness of its strength. There is no proof, statistically or otherwise, that the more "saintly" a doctor the less conscientious his care of patients, even as there is no proof either that the less "religious" a doctor the greater his efforts to excel in his profession. What is to be kept in mind is that today — and indeed in every age — Catholics must inform themselves as to what constitutes authentic Christianity and exercise good sense and sound judgment in putting it into practice.

In sum, we never outgrow the need of a more ripened view of our Christianity. We need this not so that we can join in extolling the next book on the subject of the "sacred" or "religionless Christianity." The reason goes far beyond that. In other words, every time we take a critical look at our faith, more likely than not we are confronted with a new challenge of one kind or another. We usually find that we need a deeper and clearer understanding of our own position or some rectification in the practice of what we profess. Much the same conclusion awaits us as we turn once more to Harvey Cox and the theme of secularity.

III

Harvey Cox

Cox's Christianity, is it hostile to religion? And the City of Man, does it exclude all religion? It seems not, in both cases.

The Secular City

Cox maintains that the Judeo-Christian revelation demands a secular religion, or a secularization of religion, and that this call for secularization pertains to its most distinctive contribution. Genesis "de-divinizes" nature. The Sinai Covenant "humanizes" ethics. And the Exodus represents the secularization of the State or the political structure. Cox sets the stage for and develops these points in the first chapter of *The Secular City,* appropriately titled "The Biblical Sources of Secularization." He also notes that the German theologian F. Gogarten had already advanced the same ideas. He may not have been aware of it, but in the Constitution *Gudium et Spes* Vatican II also took a position that he could applaud when it declared that

> by the very circumstance of their having been created, all things are endowed with their own stability, truth, goodness, proper laws and order. Man must respect these as he isolates them by the appropriate methods of the individual sciences or arts (no. 36).

Here then, in this declaration of the Constitution, we find indicated an aspect of secularization that could be accepted, indeed should be accepted and acted upon. On the other hand, relating the stability and goodness of the things of our world to the doctrine of creation is still a far cry from proclaiming that man should be rid of all ideologies or religious influence and that religions are destined to disappear.

Cox points to another acceptable and clear-cut aspect of secularization by the way he conceives and speaks of the Church. When "Church" definitely means "people of God," it is obvious that apart from those in holy orders or the religious state, this people is comprised of "laity," whose specific characteristic is their "secular" nature.[1] When, on the other hand, "Church" refers primarily to the "means of salvation," viz., professions of faith, sacraments, hierarchical ministry, it is again clear that this Church is by contrast and in a very special sense, not secular but "religious." Vatican Council II reaffirmed in unmistakable terms that the Church is the People of God. On this point, then, Catholics find themselves at home with Cox.

Moreover, in its discussion of the People of God (*Lumen Gentium,* chap. 2) Vatican II points out that the christian ministry and mission in the world is entrusted in the first instance to the People of God *as such.* It is the People of God as a whole that constitutes "a lasting and sure seed of unity, hope and salvation for the whole human race" (no. 9). Established by Christ, it is "used by Him as an instrument for the redemption of all" (no. 9). But we have already said that with the exception of those individuals with a special vocation this People of God is the laity, or a lay people.

When the Council sets forth the activity which the People of God are to engage in, it speaks almost entirely in religious and theological terms, holiness, redemption, common priesthood, sacramental activity, prophetic function, missionary role. What emerges is a conspectus of activities that pertain to the Church as "ordinary means of salvation" and not, or very little, to the Church as "laity living in the world." This should not surprise anyone, because every baptized person is called to play a part in the Church as "ordinary means of salvation."

---

1. See *Lumen Gentium,* no. 31.

Nevertheless — and this is the point —apart from special vocations, the People of God is the "laity," whose work and vocation is specifically "secular" (no. 31). This brings up an interesting question. If the activity of the "laity," the People of God, is set forth in terms like redemption, priesthood, prophetic mission, etc., shouldn't they be "interpreted in a secular manner" (Bonhoeffer)? And do they not relate to "careers in the world"? The question is very much to the point. In the case of one of these terms, as a matter of fact, the Council explained what it meant by it, and the explanation is "secular" in tone. The Council was speaking of the "spiritual worship" of the laity, which it proceeded to define as "their works, prayers and apostolic endeavors, their ordinary married and family life, their daily occupations, their physical and mental relaxation," provided these activities are "carried out in the Spirit" (no. 34). In other words, the Council provides us with an instance of "secular interpretation of religious concepts" (Bonhoeffer). There are any number of other religious concepts that characterize the laity, or their activity. They can also be interpreted in a secular sense, but it will take effort and imagination. Cox has made the effort, and infused it with imagination. Sometimes, it is true, he startles us by the novelty of his approach to a question. He can be caught in an extravagant mood, or with an interpretation that seems to lack foundation and is quite unacceptable. But his objective is good, his purpose right. The same kind of effort, with par. 34 of *Lumen Gentium* to guide them, is incumbent upon other Christians of the post-conciliar period.

As for the city of man, the technopolis depicted by Cox, it is not simply technological. And though it may appear to be a threat to religion, it is more properly a challenge to religion, calling upon it to revise some of its forms and structures.

Nor, in fact, is the inhabitant of the technopolis a complete robot. In describing his characteristics, viz., anonymity, mobility, "profanity," Cox points out that technological man utilizes technology precisely to guard against becoming a robot. Anonymity could conceivably result in depersonalization, but Cox notes that it also permits freer and more selective choosing of friends and leisure and social activity. Moreover, it may not be wide of the mark to see in this concern for the person and the qualitative values of life a kind of feeling or groping for God, even if techno-logical man does not quite know what name to give him. As for mobility, it has more than technological advantages. It can be, as Cox explains, a means of bringing about much sought change in one's life, and in general it makes for a more hopeful attitude towards life. In any event, the People of God is on the march, moving forward. Christian life now calls for enterprise, for bold and dynamic thrusts both as regards its spiritual dimen-sions and its externalities, the visible structure, the institutional system. Finally, when we consider the "profanity" of modern life, we may indeed find that it tends to dull man's sensitivity to the sacred, to the temple and the religious mystery. But again the outlook is not all bleak, for it is Cox's contention that the a-religious temperament of technological society permits it to dis-cover and appreciate certain values in the gospel which formerly had escaped the very people who considered themselves religious.

Cox also has definite views on ecclesiology, the theology of the Church. He wants it adapted to the age of science and tech-nology. A pivotal question is what will be the standing of the Kingdom of God in the city of man. Cox does not side with those who view the Kingdom of God as God's work and the city of man as man's. It is not possible, he says, to make this kind of separation between God's initiative on which the Kingdom of God rests and man's response to it. For, Jesus is both God and man. Like Jesus, man must be ready to take upon himself God's work and to join with God in bringing about the divine purposes. If the Kingdom of God is to progress in the world, there must be this cooperation between man and God. As a matter of fact, we are living in the eschatological age, which accounts for the world's craving for the daring and the dynamic, for renewal, for change and replacement of the old with the new. It is unlikely that Cox will win the approval of many exegetes. On the other hand, he would undoubtedly read the following lines from *Gaudium et Spes* with a great deal of interest:

> For after we have obeyed the Lord, and in his Spirit nurtured on earth the values of human dignity, brotherhood and freedom, and indeed all the good fruits of our nature and enterprise, we will find them again, but freed of stain, burnished and transfigured, when Christ hands over to the Father: "a kingdom eternal and universal, a kingdom of truth and life, of holiness and grace, of justice, love and peace." On this earth that Kingdom is already present in mystery (no. 39).

Another plea that Cox makes is for a "theology of social change," because social change is always stirring in secular life but especially in its most critical moments. He illustrates the need with a concrete case: the Cuban revolution. Christians, he notes, were simply unprepared to cope with the challenge, finding themselves "in a revolutionary situation with no theology of revolution." But the lesson of Cuba applies to the whole Christian Church, for in an age of accelerating change we still cling to a "static" theology, which obviously is not the answer to the problem of change. Nor is a theology of "history" much help, especially if it deals exclusively with the past, ignoring the present. Basically, what we need to know is this: "how is God acting for man in rapid social change?" But in developing the answer we must be careful lest we attribute to God what is not God's doing or stifle man's initiative in regard to social change and progress.

In its quest for a theology of social change theological inquiry should seek out the data of sociology and integrate them with its own data. In response to this advice, which is his own, Cox proceeds to give the "anatomy of a revolutionary theology." In every social revolution, according to Cox, four essential features are discernible:

1) the *catalytic,* which incites to action;

2) the *social catalepsy,* the failure or inability to act on the part of people who should have acted;

3) the *catharsis,* a purgative process which results in the hindrances to action being removed; and

4) the *catastrophe,* which is the "explosion" or denouement that produces the intended change by eliciting a response from those who had been unwilling or unable to act.

How does this apply to the Church, to the People of God? The catalytic factor usually appears in the form of a "catalytic gap," the lag between what is and what should be, the imbalance between one aspect of civilization and another. In the case of the Church or the Kingdom of God it appears as disagreement between the religious and cultural patterns of the pre-technical age of the past and the value systems and symbols of the modern technopolis. Or, more concretely, the God of the Bible is a God who is always a step ahead of man, beckoning him onwards, from where he is to where he has still to go. Catharsis also has its counterpart in the Bible, viz., *metanoia* or conversion, a sweeping change resulting in death of the old self and birth of the new. The catastrophe signifies the coming of the Kingdom, which is always the "coming Kingdom," never fully arrived. In every age it awakens man to the need of change, for the process of maturing, or becoming a Christian, never ends.[2]

As previously mentioned, Cox's exegesis is often extreme or "far-out" and unsubstantiated. For this reason, if for no other, the accomplished biblicist may be inclined to frown upon *The Secular City.* But be that as it may, he deserves recognition for a pioneering work of translating sociological concepts into the

---

2. The author does not identify the cataleptic aspect of the Kingdom, perhaps because it is more or less self-evident. Man, in other words, can say no to the gospel, and when he says no he fails to take the action he should take in response to it. Whatever the reason for his failure, that is the cataleptic factor. — [Tr.]

idiom of the theology of the Church, whether as institution or as People of God. Traditionally, the content of revelation has been illumined and elaborated from the perspective of a philosophy or a metaphysic. Cox's charisma is along different lines. Institutions and peoples are tangible realities which can be studied sociologically. It would seem a normal thing, then, that for purposes of ecclesiology we should also turn to scientific sociology for its contribution. Theologians readily admit this in principle but up to now have given very little evidence of it in practice. It is in this respect that Cox distinguishes himself. He introduces the sociological factor throughout his work, though with uneven results, admittedly. But the point is that those who have only criticism for his effort should try to better it, applying themselves to the task in the more rigorous and more scientific manner for lack of which (presumably) he is criticized.

An Important Afterword

The Secular City was much reviewed and discussed almost everywhere in the christian world. Some of the reviews and articles have been published under the title *The Secular City Debate*.[3] In addition to thought-provoking contributions reflecting a variety of theological opinion, there is an important Afterword by Cox himself in which, to forestall being misunderstood, he clarifies or modifies certain aspects of his position. *The Secular City,* he reminds us, began as a series of conferences to the National Student Christian Federation. Its over-all purpose was to get theologians "to open their eyes to the secular world," and the inhabitants of this secular world "to understand it and themselves in a historical-theological perspective" (p. 180). And though in general he stands by what he said in those conferences, he lets it be known that on two points in particular his thinking has undergone some

---

3. Edited by Daniel Callahan (New York and London, The Macmillan Co., 1966). Page numbers in parentheses occurring in the text refer to this work.

modification. One of these points has to do with the role of the metaphysical and the mythical element in the secular city, the other with the place of the institutional aspects of the people of God, the Church. He frankly admits that what caused him to move away from his earlier stand was not only his own experiences in the two years following the writing of the book but also the cogency of the criticism he had received.

Myth and metaphysics, he had written, are manifestations of the tribal and the town stage of societal development, implying that in the technological age they lose their significance. Now he believes they also have some real value for secular or technopolitan man. The critics, he says, who argued that ritual and cult have human significance even in a secular age were "highly persuasive" (p. 181).

The authentically mature society, he admits, even as the truly mature individual, does not throw off its past with the abandon that appears on some pages of *The Secular City*. If a society is to meet the future with courage and daring, it must accept its mythical and metaphysical past, reorganize and integrate it with a cultural identity that is open to the unpredictabilities of its future. To be sure, neither myth nor metaphysics can play the commanding role they once did, nor exercise the kind of unitive function that was theirs in the past. This does not mean, however, that "they cannot perform other humane and important functions" (p. 182). For, even though religion is a product of the tribal stage of social development, it can also have a significant place, and be a source of personal enrichment, at another stage. What should be done — and Cox promises to do — is to re-examine the specifically "religious" practices of men in order to see "what elements can be used in the interests of humanization and social change" (p. 182).

Metaphysics, too, has a place in the life of secular man. But considering what we know of the socio-cultural conditioning that enters into all philosophical speculation, it is no longer possible to look to a philosophy or a metaphysic for the representation and incarnation of the total culture of an age. Which is not to say that "metaphysics itself will die, . . . metaphysical questions can and should still be raised" (p. 186). But though the metaphysician "need not be cast on the ash heap," his role will be different, and probably nearly opposite to what it was in the past, when he exercised mainly an integrative function. In our time he will cease to be the creator of syntheses, and become the social critic, questioning the premature integrations and cultural consolidations that bind us. However, there will still be creative and integrative functions, but rather than to the metaphysician or the academic community, they will fall to the poet, cinematist, novelist and playwright.

Metaphysics, in short, is a part of man's past and therefore a part of each of us. But we should not ask it to organize and synthesize our complex universe for us. As adults, our task is to transmute the answers of classical metaphysics into questions that will maintain our openness to the world of today.

Cox's critics, by his own admission, also influenced him to modify his views regarding the organizational and institutional character of the Church (p. 186). He wants it clearly understood, however, that in *The Secular City* he never intended to be "anti-institutional, anarchistic or individualistic." He was well aware that the Church "is not a pure spirit" and that it cannot exist in the world without "some institutional expression." Nor is institution "just a necessary evil." On the contrary, it actually, serves to "liberate man rather than to imprison him" (pp. 186-187).

But this granted, Cox asks that the forms of institutional life in the Church maintain a flexibility that keeps them open to change. He gives no indication of distinguishing between what is willed by Christ or *de iure divino,* and what is demanded *only* because of the human condition. No structures, he contends, or practices are so sacred that they do not admit of change, indeed of abolition. This includes, among other things, residential parishes and the professional clergy. In this day and age there must be willingness to reinstitutionalize the forms of church life based on a conscious theological recognition of what the church's purpose is (p. 187).

Structure, in other words, must always be for a definite purpose, yet

too many of our present structures, pre-eminently the denominations, have long since outlived their usefulness and have become dysfunctional (p. 188).

Cox believes that in the Church we find a "structural fundamentalism" as well as a "biblical fundamentalism." Both are unwilling to recognize the influence of historical conditions upon the biblical text in one case and upon the structural realities of the Church in the other.

But Cox is not discouraged. He sees signs of hope, as in the willingness of some people to re-examine and, if need be, to change traditional patterns of church life, and in the growing tendency to regard the structural apparatus of the Church as a means of serving the cause of peace and justice in the world rather than as an instrumentality for bolstering the status of the Church itself (p. 188). Vatican II is cited to show how much indeed ecclesiastical structures can be changed and transformed. But alas! too many Church organizations remain self-centered and immobile.

Such, in sum, is Cox's updated thinking concerning the place of myth, metaphysics and the institutional Church in the secular city. All told, his thought is more profound and more intricate than some passages in *The Secular City* — those that are most often cited — would lead one to believe. Thanks, moreover, to dialogue and reconsideration that followed its publication, "myth" and the "religious" and "institutional" assume importance again. It is gratifying to note this, for an author's honesty is always appreciated.

IV

"De-sacralization" and "Secularity"

In the introduction to this study we called attention to Pope Paul VI's allocution in which he spoke of the "not negligible portion of truth" that may be discovered in ideas as novel and ambivalent as are propagated by advocates of "de-sacralization." It is still too early to ascertain all the constructive aspects of this intriguing phenomenon. As for its immoderate or irresponsible tendencies, we shall not dwell on them. Better to take stock of the progress it has made and perhaps benefit from it.

"De-sacralization"

As we have seen, this movement seeks the "reinforcement" of temporal values and opposes any ideological or institutional influence which it deems obstructive of its goal. Its advocates appear to be in good company, for contemporary Catholic theology is oriented in the same general direction, and Vatican II documents dealing with the Church's relation to the world have much the same end in view.

In its pastoral Constitution *Gaudium et Spes* (no. 36) the Council gives unqualified endorsement to the "autonomy" of earthly realities, declaring that these realities — human societies and sciences in particular — have their proper laws, proper consistence and proper excellence. This autonomy is not tolerated or suffered, but accords with the positive will of the Creator. God does not place man in a world to which he may be indifferent, or which is of no importance to him. Man should understand that in God's design every domain of earthly affairs has its truth, its consistence, its proper activity.

The Council's statement on the autonomy of earthly realities

is particularly explicit in regard to the sciences and scientific
investigation, whatever the branch of knowledge under study.
The Galileo case is in point. Much ink has been spilled over it,
and whenever charges of obscurantism are leveled against the
Church, this regrettable affair is likely to be trotted out. The
Council, as a matter of fact, was petitioned for the rehabilitation
of Galileo. The request came from many quarters, but especially
from Catholic university groups, who felt it was an opportune
moment because the fourth anniversary of his birth (b. 1464) fell
within the span of the Council's sessions. Bishop Elchinger made
the proposal to the Fathers.[1] After several revisions the Council,
in a toned down statement, settled for an allusion to the Galileo
incident in deploring "certain habits of mind, which are sometimes found too among Christians, which do not sufficiently attend to the rightful independence of science" (no. 36).

But the Council, as we have seen, also declares that man is
to "relate" all things to God, for their purpose is not exhausted
in serving man. In referring them to God he acknowledges their
higher purpose, their ultimate function. How is this "reference"
to be construed? Obviously not in the same sense that would nul-
lify everything the Council says regarding the excellence and
autonomy, or the rightful independence of created realities, especially of man and his will and activity.

And yet, this is the interpretation we sometimes find. Earthly
realities are thought to be mere means, or instruments and tools
(*machinae*), deriving value and importance only from being referred or offered to God. In themselves they are not true or praise-
worthy; it is their "ordination" to God that makes them such. This
outlook was characteristic, not of the main branch of Augustinian-
ism but of its excrescences and carried over into the spiritual life
and, in some degree, to christian life generally. If, then, the things
of this world are to have any goodness or truth, in the Augustinian
sense, they must be "offered to God" or placed "at the service
of divine worship and praise." This attitude is not altogether

---

1. *Docum. cathol.* December 20, 1964, coll. 1662-1665.

a thing of the past. It still exists, in books yes, but mostly in the mentality of certain Christians. But the generality of Christians, especially that vast majority who are fully occupied with secular activity, are not persuaded of it.

That all things should be referred to God no one questions. Vatican II reiterates the principle. But the Council's meaning is far different. In its view earthly realities — those, obviously, which represent sound values and are assumable by a Christian — they do indeed have their own consistence, an existential "solidity," which is to say a kind of self-existence, though (we should hasten to add) not in the sense that we speak of God's self-existence. But all that said, we have also to take cognizance of their transcendent significance, their ultimate dimension, which requires that they be "referred" to God — referred by man, who discovers them, reduces and rejoices in them. Primarily, man does this in his heart, through an inner act or attitude by which he acknowledges God as the beginning and the end of all things. Man living his life to capacity, facing the world unperturbed, taking in stride his family, his work, his leisure and rest, all as God wills, all for God: such is the outlook of the Council, the gist of its "ordering" of all things to God.

As for rejecting whatever tends to hinder the movement toward "de-sacralization," this is only logical if the movement itself has any validity. Christian theology is also opposed to such hindrances. It does not accept an "image of the world" in which "nature" and the "divine" are inextricably interwoven; where natural forces are "explained" by adducing some divine power; where through incantations priests think they can appease divinities or render them propitious; where man regards himself as the victim of blind fate, of inexorable necessity or an inescapable providence that decrees and administers every detail of his life. It is an image that has indeed been discredited, principally by the positive sciences, whose discoveries have led to the extrusion of the mystical or magical element from essentially natural and human phenomena. But modern philosophy has also had a hand in it, by its persistent attack on this "religious" image of the world, a legacy of the primitive age of religion and philosophy.

The extent to which this image has been shattered is suggested by Vatican II's attitude. The Council virtually ignores it. In fact, if it can be said to have taken note of it at all, it would be in the parenthetical observation that "many benefits once looked for, especially from heavenly powers, man has now enterprisingly procured for himself." [2] By contrast, the Council lays much stress on what in current parlance is referred to as human "creativity," declaring among other things that "man, created to God's image, received a mandate to subject to himself the earth and all it contains, and to govern the world with justice and holiness." [3] It also affirms that "when a man works he not only alters things and society, he develops himself as well." [4] And it begins its consideration of the proper development of culture with this un-equivocal declaration: "Man comes to a true and full humanity only through culture, that is through the cultivation of the goods and values of nature. Wherever human life is involved, therefore, nature and culture are quite intimately connected one with the other." [5]

On the other hand, the idea of "creative activity" on the part of man does pose some problems both for the theologian and the philosopher. Foremost is the question of second (i.e., created) causes. Can the First Cause produce second causes that are causes in the true sense of the word, real and autonomous and distinct from Itself? Much has been, and will continue to be, written on this subject, seeing that freedom is the key to the authenticity and autonomy of human activity, the cornerstone that sustains the edifice. But can the actuality of man's freedom be maintained if it is totally dominated by the transcendence and omniscience of God? [6]

---

2. *Gaudium et Spes*, no. 33.
3. *Ibid.*, no. 34.
4. *Ibid.*, no. 35.
5. *Ibid.*, no. 53.
6. For the quoted material in the following paragraphs relative to this

On this question, two basic views share the debate. Many theologians and philosophers hold to a form of "predeterminism." According to this view, "the universal order and all its defects, and the actual history of the created world, would pre-exist completely in the Creative Thought [scil. of God]." Otherwise (it is argued,) God would be a mere "spectator" of human history and his providence would be conditioned by the free decisions of creatures — suppositions that contradict God's immutability and omniscience. Hence it must be said that "my free acts are predetermined in the Creative Cause." This, however (or so runs the argument), does not jeopardize the reality of man's freedom, because "creation is not a *motion;* hence I am not 'pushed' to will in spite of myself."

This explanation has much in its favor, and many metaphysicians accept it. But it should be remembered that it is a theological explanation, not an article of the Catholic faith, so that other answers to this question are possible, answers in which human freedom is perhaps allotted a greater role yet without prejudice to God's transcendence.

One alternative to predeterminism is, for want of a better term, a kind of *indeterminism.* It, too, has many supporters, including Thomists. In their opinion, if the freedom of the creature is to have any meaning at all, it must be absolute or unconditioned, even in regard to the First Cause. Only on this supposition is it possible to account for moral evil, which either emanates from the human will alone, or else it must also be imputed to God. Here is where predeterminism comes to grief, for despite protestations to the contrary, it does in fact amount to absolute determinism. For, under that system, not only would the history of the world be reduced to an inexorable unrolling of a plan already fixed by God in every detail, but "the worst crimes committed by created persons would be known, willed, and caused by God before they were willed by secondary causes."

question, see F. van Steenberghen, *Ontology,* 210-216 (for translator, etc., see Part II, chap. 2, note 6).

As a matter of fact (continuing the argument), the principles on which predeterminism rests are not as invulnerable as is claimed. Indeed, they suggest a faulty understanding of certain attributes of God, such as omnipotence and transcendence. God's omnipotence finds its highest expression in the creation of persons who are truly free, truly capable of determining themselves and their own destiny. If God uses this marvelous power to create such beings who are truly free, it is "He Himself who deliberately introduces something contingent and unforeseeable into His own handiwork," and he forfeits nothing of his omnipotence by accepting the consequences of his creative act. As for the divine transcendence or immutability, neither of these is incompatible with God's knowing our free decisions at the moment we make them, for he knows them "by reason of His presence in the innermost being of created substances, as their permanent Creative Cause"; which is to say he knows them in a manner which, properly speaking, "excludes all passivity and and all receptivity." (Thus the indeterminists.)

As we have indicated, indeterminism can claim the support of many philosophers and theologians, perhaps more than formerly. All in all, it appears to be a more exact statement than predeterminism of the unfathomable mystery in which God's foreknowledge is somehow reconciled with the freedom of man's will. But however that may be, we want it understood that in discussing the two positions we limited ourselves to the order of creation or the natural order. A complete account must also take into consideration the supernatural or the order of grace, for this "entails a special providence on the part of God which profoundly affects the data of the problem." This special providence includes divine interventions which can direct the course of history as willed by God, with or without the co-operation of the will of his creatures.

But whichever it is that we prefer, predeterminism or indeterminism, it would be absurd to conclude that because of his freedom and autonomy "the rational creature exists as a kind of rival to the Creator" (*Gaudium et Spes,* no. 34). The Promethean myth has no place in the christian setting. Man is not a Titan chained to a rock for having plundered fire from heaven and with it the rudiments of civilization. Nor is our God a Zeus who can be robbed of his mystery. He is more transcendent, and more generous too, creating us free and with a capacity for creative activity, which he wills us to exercise in every segment of life and the world, and with his help to be vigorous and effective in the exercise of it. That is why tomorrow's world may well be different in structure and appearance from today's, why christian life in the world can project a new image to each generation. Christians have not to tremble before a jealous Jupiter. Their God knows not jealousy. It is by his leave, rather at his behest that they embark upon every human enterprise. And it is to enterprise that the Council summons them when it notes that "the triumphs of the human race are a sign of God's grace and the flowering of His own mysterious design." [7]

"Secularity"

"Secularity" is here used in the untainted sense, as equivalent to Pope Pius XII's expression, "sound laicity of the State." [8] Vatican Council II, particularly in *Lumen Gentium* and *Gaudium et Spes,* sets forth the christian ideal for the generality of Christians.[9] Though this ideal is secular in character, its ultimate reference, its final end and purpose, is theological and is assured through the *ecclesiastical* ministry of sanctification.

The doctrinal lines of this secular conception are drawn in that part of *Lumen Gentium* which deals with the "common priesthood" of the faithful. In our earlier consideration of this part we pointed out that in Catholic theology, and even in the Conciliar documents, we find instances of "secular interpretation

---

7. *Gaudium et Spes,* no. 34.
8. "Come si la legittima *sana laicità dello Stato* non fosse uno dei principi della dottrina cattolica" (*L'Osservatore Romano*, March 24-25, 1948).
9. As compared with those with a special vocation, i.e., the ministry or the life of the evangelical counsels, the so-called "religious" life.

of religious notions." We now propose, in the light of the same passages to trace the "secular" pattern in its total perspective, or as it relates to the "laity" and their christian life as a whole.

The capital passage in this respect is the following:

> All their works, prayers and apostolic endeavors, their ordinary married and family life, their daily occupations, their physical and mental relaxation, if carried out in the Spirit, and even the hardships of life, if patiently borne — all these become "spiritual sacrifices acceptable to God through Jesus Christ" [1 Pet. 2:5] (no. 34).

This, in essence, is a sketch of integral christian living. Family, work, leisure, devotional practice, these are the ingredients, the raw materials that enter into "spiritual worship," the worship "in Spirit" that characterizes the New Covenant, the gospel of Jesus Christ. "Spiritualization of worship," as it is sometimes put, is indeed a mark of the New Testament, but this does not simply mean that its worship or religion is more "interior." Rather the meaning is that the totality of the Christian's daily life (family, occupation, leisure, prayer life), every word and deed, if performed in and in harmony with the Spirit, is to be regarded as worship, in the first sense of the word.

No doubt, there are Christians who are not aware of this, or not sufficiently. Their idea of New Testament worship is exclusively sacramental, and the common priesthood of the faithful, as they understand it, consists entirely in receiving certain sacraments or joining in the Eucharistic worship.[10] Clearly, some updating, *aggiornamento*, is in order here. The conception which these Christians have of "spiritual worship" needs to be replaced with a conception that is not exclusively sacramental, which is to say it needs "de-sacralization." For, as we have repeatedly said, spiritual worship consists of more than sacraments; it consists

---

10. *Lumen Gentium*, no. 11, describes the sacramental aspect of the common priesthood of the faithful.

also of the Christian's work or profession, his married and family life, his leisure and diversion, all these when pursued in and in harmony with the Spirit.

But then, what happens to the sacramental life? Is it abolished? A rhetorical question, obviously. For the sacramental life is, as it were, the ecclesial masculature, the prop and support, of "worship in the Spirit." And *Lumen Gentium* does not overlook it. Immediately joined to the excerpt from par. 34 is a statement in which the sacramental function is organically related to the christian life:

> Together with the offering of the Lord's body, they [the "spiritual sacrifices": family, work, leisure, devotional life] are most fittingly offered in the celebration of the Eucharist.

As for its "secular" interpretation of the christian ideal, the Constitution had already indicated in par. 10, where the common priesthood of the faithful is under discussion:

> The baptized, by regeneration and the anointing of the Holy Spirit, are consecrated as a spiritual house and a holy priesthood, in order that *through all those works which are those of the christian man (per omnia opera hominis christiani)* they may offer spiritual sacrifices . . . .

The Constitution uses the term "consecrated" to indicate the direct effect of the sacrament of baptism but the results of this consecration are termed "spiritual house" and "holy priesthood." And when it speaks of "spiritual sacrifices," it intends the total activity of daily life pursued in and in conformance with the Spirit.[11]

Turning to the topic of holiness (chap. V), the Council Fathers continue to develop this "secular" orientation of the

---

11. See also Yves M. J. Congar, *Laity, Church, and World,* pp. 181-221, 379-428; trans. Donald Attwater (Baltimore, Helicon Press, 1961).

christian life. There is but one holiness, to which all are called but each according to his temporal situation, his walk of life, in short his particular vocation (nos. 39-40). In all its forms, holiness is not a question of crying "Lord, Lord" but doing the will of the Father epitomized in love of God and neighbor (no. 42). For the Christian, his daily life and activities represent this "practice" of love which is the "means" of holiness. But, apart from the ministry of the religious life, "daily" existence consists precisely of the things which the Constitution had set forth in par. 34: prayer and the apostolate, conjugal and family life, work and leisure, all in all an existence that is far more "secular" than "religious." Yet it is in the "activities" of this largely secular existence that love of God and neighbor, whereby we become holy, assumes concrete form and expression.

The Council's "secular" thrust, for that matter, was not altogether without precedent. It had been anticipated to a large extent by St. Francis de Sales. Indeed, if the principles he develops in the *Introduction to the Devout Life* were taken seriously by Christians, they would be well on the way toward realizing the ideal of christian life that emerges from the Constitutions *Lumen Gentium* and *Gaudium et Spes*. Writes the saint:

> St. Joseph, Lydia and St. Crispin were perfectly devout *in the workshop;* St. Anne, St. Martha, St. Monica, Aquila, Priscilla *in their homes;* Cornelius, St. Sebastian, St. Maurice *in the army;* Constantine, Helen, St. Louis, Blessed Amadeus and St. Edward *in the courts.* It has even happened that many have fallen away in solitude, in itself so conducive to perfection, and preserved their virtue *in the midst of crowds,* which are [supposedly] unconducive to it.[12]

Compared with some earlier schools of spirituality, the teaching of St. Francis represented a clear secularization of the chris-

---

12. *Introduction to the Devout Life,* part I, chap. 3, pp. 14-15; trans. by Michael Day (Westminster, Md., The Newman Press, 1959).

tian ideal. However, his ideas found little immediate acceptance, nor was their significance generally appreciated. For centuries it had been thought that "geographical" separation from the "world" was a requirement for the pursuit of perfection, and that the "virtuous" life was not normally possible in a "secular" environment. Spirituality was written and preached by persons who had left the world, for vocation's sake. Actually, it is only recently that the proposition that every legitimate form of life and activity could have sanctifying value has received practical and widespread recognition. *Lumen Gentium,* a dogmatic constitution, is obviously in support of it. It is indeed God who makes us holy, but he accomplishes it through man's fulfillment of his state of life, hence through man's occupation, through his family concerns, his rest and leisure, as well as through his prayer life and apostolic activities. The one condition: that he live "in the Spirit."

And yet is it not true that we should "always pray"? Hausherr has studied this question in the Church Fathers, with the following result:

Agreement is complete among the three segments of Christianity: Greek with Origen, Semitic with Aphraates, Latin with Augustine. All agree that to pray always is to pray at certain times of the day and between this moment or hours of explicit prayer to do only good works, which will be an implicit prayer. Origen is the only one who says that that is the only way to have continuous prayer. The others do not say this but obviously presuppose it, since it goes without saying, once we rule out the Messalian fiction of life spent in unbroken vocal or mental prayer, with all mundane activity forbidden. To be determined, however, are the conditions under which manual or intellectual labor takes on the value of prayer.[13]

---

13. I. Hausherr, "La Prière perpétuelle du chrétien," in the collective work *Sainteté et Vie dans le siècle,* p. 127 (Rome, Herder, 1965). Messalianism: "the doctrine of a christian sect which arose about 350

It is not necessary, continues Hausherr, to intersperse our "profane" activities with pious thoughts, in a constant shift of attention from one to the other. We have only to be properly disposed as a matter of course, cultivating an inner rectitude and righteousness. It is not a question, then, of "a thought superimposed upon our activity; rather it is something that penetrates the activity itself, something that influences, directs and determines it." [14]

> The secret of being in continuous prayer is not in introducing to work the adjunct of prayer, something extraneous to it, but in transforming work itself into prayer by viewing it in its whole reality here and now and in its veritable finality. That is the only way, says St. Basil, to avoid distraction and to maintain some kind of unity within oneself. It is also the only way to reconcile the two precepts of the Apostle: "Pray without ceasing" (I Thess. 5:17) and, in effect, "Work night and day" (II Thess. 3:8). [15]

Holiness, then, lies in the bond of charity, of christian love, which is forged in the crucible of daily existence, the totality of daily activity comprising family, work, rest, prayer. In proportion as the clergy confuse the utilization of the "ecclesiastical means" of sanctification with the personal act of theological love, which is first and fundamental, there is need of reappraisal, need for

---

A.D. (also known as Euchites, Enthusiasts, etc.) that Christians should abstain from work and the sacraments as unprofitable for the desired experience of grace, and can attain the beatific vision even in this life through asceticism. It was widespread in Asia Minor and was condemned by several synods and the Council of Ephesus (A.D. 431)" (Rahner-Vorgrimler, *Theological Dictionary*, p. 286; trans. Richard Stracham [New York, Herder and Herder, 1965. London, Burns & Oates]). See also *Catholic Encyclopedia*, old edition. – [Tr.]

14. *Op. cit.*, p. 134.
15. *Op. cit.*, p. 142.

a revision of values which will result in the principal emphasis being put where it belongs, on the personal act of love. This love is nurtured and strengthened in the temporal vocation, in meeting the duties and responsibilities of one's state of life. The ecclesiastical means of sanctification must remain what they are intended to be: "means." If the means (presence in church, e.g.) are accorded precedence over the end in view (love, in all aspects of life), then a certain "de-clericalization" of the spiritual life is in order. We might even call it "de-sacralization," if there is question of dispelling the notion that man becomes holy only through the ecclesiastical means, and not through his so-called "profane" life, the pursuit of his profession and the care of his family. We could even entertain the suggestion of a "less religious christian spirituality," if this means a doctrine of spirituality that does indeed stress the importance of prayer but also, in fact most of all, inculcates the sanctifying value of "non-religious" activities, such as fill up most of the day for the body of Christians.

Inspiring this view of the christian life which we have been discussing is, as to be expected, an eschatological outlook that also bears the stamp of "secularity." But this demands some explanation.

Perhaps we should begin with a question, viz., "what kind of existence is in store for the 'community of the elect' after the resurrection, when body and soul shall have been united again?" About this, it must be confessed, we know next to nothing, since revelation is almost totally silent regarding the "eschatological mystery." *Almost,* for christian theology has been able to put together some vague notions on the subject, and these of course we can repeat. But that does not mean that we have "realized" or penetrated the reality of the mystery. It is as with a child that keeps saying he will be a man some day. What he says is true but he cannot "realize' what it means to be a man. In the case of heaven we keep trying, in spite of ourselves, to imagine the thing. And we imagine badly, and generally to the detriment of realities suggested by expressions like "earthly values" or "secular realities."

There is, for example, the picture of "heaven as ecstasy." Christians read about great saints who were favored with the highest mystical experiences, including the ecstatic rapture, which transported them to the "seventh heaven." Believing that ecstasy is as though the portal to heavenly bliss, what more natural than to conclude that they too, having expiated their faults, will be transported into a kind of super-ecstasy, forever? It is a recognized fact, however, that in the ecstatic experience both the inner and outer senses are virtually "bound." The soul is conscious of its spiritual union with God. Every other awareness is suspended. If this is heaven, a kind of super-ecstasy, it is clear that so-called "temporal realities" — and this includes the senses — have no part in it. But in that event what purpose or meaning is left to them? This heaven, in effect, reduces them to pseudo-realities, existing only for the here and now and in principle already abolished. But is that really what heaven is?

There is also the picture of "heaven as liturgy." The rich imagery of the Apocalypse, as in the glorious vision of chapters 5 and 22, suggests a splendorous liturgy in ceaseless enactment through the everlasting age. This heaven is the glorification of the virtue of "religion," of which ecclesiastical liturgies, those of religious communities in particular, are deemed a preview and foretaste. It is a heaven in which cultual and ecclesiastical values, such as are especially cultivated by the clergy and religious, are duly recognized. But as for nonsacred values, the "profane" in the current acceptation, these to all intents and purposes are completely ignored. If this be the final condition of man, his earthly existence has very little meaning. For by far the greater part of this existence is "profane," dealing with secular realities, in the secular world, which the Council explicitly characterizes as the special province of the laity. Unless this aspect of man's temporal condition enters into his final condition, it has value only for the moment, which is to say it is all but meaningless.

The Constitution *Gaudium et Spes* beckons us to a different

view of man's final existence. To be sure, the spiritual and mystical component remains primary, that which "eye hath not seen
nor ear heard" (I Cor. 2:9) and can neither be denied nor
diminished, but it will be accompanied by physical and communal
elements. We are assured of the physical integrity of the person,
by reason of the power of God's kingdom. The prodigies and
wonders of this world may be read as intimations of the new earth
and the new heavens to come. Even now, as we walk this earth,
anticipations of the Kingdom are discernible where the harmony
of true community prevails because justice and peace and freedom reign, which are "fruits of the Spirit." Working in the Spirit,
to the extent of our capacities, we promote the growth of "the
body of a new human family," a body that is also "some kind
of foreshadowing of the new age." [16] The great diversity of human
values implied in the term "progress" are like so many human
assets which a benevolent God can welcome into the Kingdom.
Not that technical progress is the measuring rod of the quality
of the Kingdom. *That* would be the worst delusion of all. Yet
"the values of human dignity, brotherhood and freedom, and
indeed all the good fruits of our nature and enterprise, we will find
them again," — not as before, but unstained, brightened, trans-
figured — when in his risen glory the Lord hands over to his
Father a Kingdom of love and peace.

Compared with heaven as ecstasy or liturgy, the heaven of
Gaudium et Spes is far more receptive of the whole of reality and
to this extent represents a kind of "de-sacralization." This is a
point of capital importance, for in the ascertainment of the true
form of christian life in this world, the life of the world to come,
the eschatological factor, is the most decisive and most illumina-
ting consideration.

---

16. *Gaudium et Spes,* no. 39; same reference for the citation that follows.

Conclusion

The demand for a "religionless" Christianity does not want for greatness — the greatness of ambivalence. In Dietrich Bonhoeffer the ambivalence is almost heart-rending. It takes greatness to be in prison and, in the face of uncertainty and threats and bombs raining down at any hour, to say what Bonhoeffer says in these lines:

> I therefore want to start from the premise that God should not be smuggled into some last secret place, but that we should frankly recognize that the world, and people, have come of age, that we should not run man down in his worldliness, but confront him with God at his strongest point.[1]

And it takes greatness, great courage, for anyone in the precarious circumstances of Bonhoeffer to come to the defense of "earthly realities" and write glowing pages about Beethoven's music, the Italian sun, the German poets, the Roman galleries: this the more that according to Bonhoeffer's theology these penultimate or "before the last" things, as he calls them, though they may continue to exist after the resurrection, are not therefore "sanctioned" by it.[2]

In the *Ethics* Bonhoeffer has some thoroughly thoughtful chapters on the meaning and purpose of earthly realities, which are "before the last" both qualitatively and chronologically. The problem of the relation between the "last" things and things which

---

1. *Letters and Papers from Prison,* pp. 192-3.
2. See *Ethics,* pp. 125-143; trans. Neville Horton Smith (London, S. M. C. Press, 1966. Fontana Library paperback).

are "before the last" has its solution in Jesus Christ, the incarnate, crucified and risen God. For in Christ, "the reality of God meets the reality of the world," and in Christ we share in "this real encounter." Bonhoeffer's judgment as to the inmost meaning of things which are penultimate or "before the last" depends on his view of the final condition of risen man. This man, in effect, "remains man, even though he is a new, a risen man, who in no way resembles the old man."[3]

Bonhoeffer is both deeply religious and deeply "nonreligious." And there lies the ambivalence, the paradox and contradiction. Bonhoeffer, prophet of the "nonreligious," is the same Bonhoeffer who believes in God, in Christ; who believes in sin and the grace of reconciliation; believes in his pastoral ministry and the saving power of the preached Word; believes also in baptism, communion and confession, and in prayer, even the prayer of "intercession." [4] Those who feel they cannot overlook the occasional outburst, the intemperate remark or disquieting thought, they ought at least to have the honesty not to betray the man himself. It is important that Bonhoeffer be understood correctly — his critics owe him that much, at the very least. For the rest, when we speak of the substantivity and the autonomy of earthly realities, it ought to be done in a positive manner. Negative terms like "nonreligious" or "irreligious" smack of polemics, and besides, it is only in the context of "secularity" that they have any real significance.

Regarding conclusions to be drawn from our study, there we find ourselves rather at a loss. Summary and synthesis in this case are not easy to distill. Nevertheless, we shall make an attempt.

Before anything else, may we say that the abuse and/or commercialization, as we see today, of the terms "irreligious" and "de-sacralized" and others like them is a deplorable spectacle. It is deplorable because it strikes at the most sensitive fibres of the human heart with a certain brutality that betrays a lack of human kindness and apparently knows no shame. And it is harmful

---

3. See *ibid.*, pp. 130-133.
4. See *Letters and Papers from Prison*, pp. 214, 215.

and corruptive because it fails to discriminate. Sound insights and representations which deserve to be reckoned with are put on the same level as assertions which are outrageously arrogant or irreverent and would in some case be unmitigated blasphemy were it not for the dedication and sincerity of those who make them. But perhaps most regrettable is that it plays into the hands of those — and they are still with us — who seize every occasion or opportunity to undermine the cause of God and religion and the Church.

The basic problem stems from the variety of meanings in the terms "sacred" and "religious." It is not uncommon, of course, for a term to have several meanings, as any dictionary will show, and in our case it accounts for the fact that most of the time a demand for de-sacralization cannot be met with a flat "yes or no" but only with "yes *and* no." Compounding the problem, moreover, is that a discussion of "religious-vs-nonreligious" Christianity or "sacred-vs-profane" existence usually involves other more or less antithetical notions which also suffer from lack of uniform and precise theological formulation, such as created and re-created, nature and grace, world and revelation, city and Church, daily life and holiness, people of God and kingdom of God. In any debate a definition of terms is essential to fruitful discussion. In our case the participants have first to agree on the meaning of "sacred" and "religious," keeping in mind that the meaning can be influenced by historical circumstances and the cultural environment.

On the whole, it appears that the conception of authentic christian life is due for some modification. The *form* of this life will become, in fact is already becoming "less religious." There are many indications of this change, apart from the theological ferment of the times and the turbulent impatience of some Christians. We see a genuine acceptance of the inherent substantiality and the autonomy of earthly realities. We find also an acknowldgment of human creativity, freely and responsibly exercised. Indicative, too, are the "secular" conception of the common priesthood and the recognition that every state of life is conducive to holiness, that it can and should be achieved by the laity in their "secular" condition. Even the consecrated life, all along the line, from monasticism to "secular" institutes, is undergoing a certain transformation. Finally, not without significance in this regard are recent discussions on the final condition of man after the resurrection. To this extent, then, "secularity" is already the way of life for the People of God. They themselves, the People of God, will provide the practical solution to the problem we have examined in this study, following it through the theological literature that has occupied our attention. They will provide it in their daily living, in their attitudes and outlook. And what is the proper solution? A "nonreligious" Christianity? No. What then, a "less religious" form of Christianity? Yes. But the question then is: how is this "less religious" Christianity to be conceived? Some thoughts along this line follow.

The "world," to begin with the fundamentals of any solution, is God's creation. All that we are, all that we call the universe, was created by him, "maker of heaven and earth, and of all things visible and invisible" (Creed). This means that the "created" is radically and essentially dependent on God. It is dependent on him not in this or that respect but in every respect, in all of its being. More concisely and in different terms, the creature is *relative* to God, completely. This relation, however, does not destroy the "consistence," the self-containing character of the creature but rather accounts for and saves it. "Creation is pure relation and unilateral relation as regards the reality of things, . . . this condition establishes the creature in the most perfect existential and functional autonomy." [5]

Now, to identify the creature *as relative to God,* is it necessary to introduce the term "sacred." We think not. In fact, it would be inadvisable wherever it conjured up the idea that some things are "sacred in themselves" and others "profane in themselves."

---

5. A. D. Sertillanges, *L'Idée de création et ses retentissements en philosophie,* p. 59 (Paris, Aubier, 1945).

Yet we need not go so far as to rule out the term altogether, as in expressions like "sacred mystery of the creature." What decides here, as in many other circumstances, is the context in which a statement is made and the cultural formation of those who hear or otherwise learn of it.

The same reply, in our opinion, holds for the term "religious" or "religion." We do not feel that in order to identify the creature *as relative to God* it is necessary to have recourse to these terms. What is necessary is to understand what is meant by "dependence of being." Some regard this expression, "dependence of being," as a more adequate and more searching designation for the "relativeness" of the creature than the term "religious." In any event, the important thing is not the terminology but the reality, or rather, understanding the reality, namely of the relation. For that matter, the terms "religious" and "religion" can also convey the idea of essential dependence. The way they are used in Barth and Durkheim is not the only way.

In the view of some Christians, not only is it not necessary to employ the term "sacred" or "religion" to designate the transcendental relation of creational dependence, but at the present time, and, perhaps at any time, it is preferable not to use them. Avoiding these terms, they say, is the best way to maintain the authentic conception of this relation from the Christian point of view. Their reasons should be taken into account. Their great concern is of course to prevent the taint of syncretism from creeping into the christian idea of the creational relation. But, in all frankness, they would serve their own purpose better if they declared their mind more freely and more explicitly.

This same creation which is dependent upon God for its being is also dependent upon him for its sanctification. This entire creation — man and the universe — is to be "sanctified" through the gratuitous gift of holiness that comes from God, the Holy One par excellence. "You alone are holy!" Every creature, then, and each according to the mode of its being, is called to share in the holiness of God. His holiness is not simply one of many divine attributes. It characterizes God as such and comprises all "the abundance of life, all the power and goodness" [6] that God represents. To participate in God's holiness is, in a way, to be unceasingly re-born in consequence of God's unbroken operation in the creature.

This new condition, a spiritually vitalizing condition, is called justification or sanctification. And it raises the same question. Must we call it "sacred"? And again the answer is no; it is not necessary. In fact, "sacred" as understood by Durkheim does not apply to it at all, since all creation is destined to become a new creature. Here as elsewhere, the context of what is said or written will often determine whether "sacred" is advisable or not.

But sanctification, which signifies participation in everything that the power and the goodness of God comprises, if it need not be called "sacred," should it be called "religious"? Definitely not, if or to the extent that religion is considered a human enterprise, man's work. Sanctification is God's gift, even as is faith when it refers to the supernatural event of reconciliation. Nor would "religious" be proper if it were to lend credence to the idea that participation in God's holiness must assume the form of prayer or worship, when as a matter of fact it can be realized in all human activity and in every situation. Since that is the case, why not say, as *Lumen Gentium* in effect says, that daily work and rest are "spiritual offerings," part and parcel of worship under the New Covenant?

Those Christians who feel that "sacred" and "religious" should never be used in reference to the "sanctification" of mankind and the world can produce sound and noteworthy reasons. And perhaps there is some significance in the fact that the current expression for this sanctification is not "sacred grace" or "religious grace" but "sanctifying grace." Even so, these same Christians could tell us more clearly what is behind their diffidence, what it is they object to, and how far their objections go. How they con-

---

6. See art. "Saint," *Vocabulaire de theologie biblique,* col. 983 (Paris, Éd. du Cerf, 1962).

ceive this nonreligious or nonsacred sanctification of mankind and the world? What, precisely, is the hitch to the terms "religious" and "sacred"? And their rejection of them, is it temporary and prudential, aimed at clearing the air of misunderstandings, or is it doctrinal and final, because the terms as such are inaccurate and inadmissible? Meanwhile, it might be well to remind ourselves that the discussion of terms does not affect the reality one way or another.

Man, a creature, has somehow to acknowledge his creatural condition, has also to respond to the gift of sanctification. How does he do this? He does it in private, certainly. Above all and just as certainly, he does it in spirit, interiorly. But he also does it with his whole self, in an external manner that but reflects the acceptance in the heart. This external response embraces a variety of rites and ceremonies, of practices and doctrines of which Christ himself is the essential author. Yet without adequate "human space" nothing human comes off as it should. The Christian, in other words, plants his personal acceptance within the heart of a community, within a Church, "ordinary means of salvation," which must have enough "terrestrial space" to function normally. Both Barth and Bonhoeffer admit there must be such "space," such "place," even though they may not attach as much theological weight to it as Catholic theologians. Regarding this space and place, the same question arises: Are they "sacred"? Are they "religious"?

The Church, without a doubt, is first of all the people of God, the community of Christians, the Eucharistic assembly. But it is also, in a very real sense, "ordinary means" of praise and sanctification. Our Lord has given us a gospel of holiness. He instituted rites of sanctification. He established a community of believers. These realities of the doctrinal and ritual and institutional order are "ecclesial" and "ecclesiastical." They constitute a human "space," a human "place."

These "means of sanctification," are they "sacred"? Use of the term in this connection is certainly not indispensable. "Ecclesiastical" or "ecclesial" will generally do. And indeed, "sacred" is better avoided where it would only inspire the notion of realities "sacred in themselves," as understood by Durkheim. When the term *is* applied to the means of sanctification proper to the ecclesiastical institution, we should make it very clear what we intend by it. For, even though man's "profane" existence (work, leisure, family life, etc.), if carried on in the Spirit, is a fundamental means of sanctification, the unfortunate impression could be created — and often is, sometimes deliberately — that this means does not command the same esteem as those administered by the Church, i.e., the ecclesiastical institution. Yet the term "sacred" is not objectionable in principle as a descriptive for the means of sanctification that are properly "ecclesiastical," i.e., administered by the Church. It would be especially appropriate to means of the ritual order.

These "means of sanctification," are they "religious"? Here we must weigh matters even more carefully. They are not religious in the Barthian sense, for their efficacy is entirely God's gift. God is the sole Source of all sanctification, the only Name with power to save. Still, these means are intended for the community of the Lord's faithful. They are bonds, signs, instruments which by their very institution are associated with God's gift to man and man's union with God. Is not that a very "religious" value? That a term can be abused is no reason for going to the other extreme — no use at all.

As we have seen, there are any number of questionable attitudes and "religious" conceptions among Christians which could account, at least in part, for the demand for a "nonreligious" intepretation of christian existence in the world and for the world. However, there may be something more basic behind it all, a discernment of the Church as a "sign of the times," today perhaps more than in the past. We know it by faith and revelation that the Church is tending toward the Kingdom. We know, too, the importance for the Church of this vibrant, this living relationship with the Kingdom.

The Church is already the Kingdom of heaven, the Kingdom

in the process of constitution. This process continues till the
end of time, when the only remaining requirement for the
completion of the Kingdom will be that the external form of
this world disappear and the true reality which it hides be
unveiled throughout. The Church is the Kingdom of God,
which lacks only the light that will reveal what is now hidden.
It is not possible to conceive of a Church in the true sense
yet existing independently of the Kingdom of God, of its
fulfillment, its purpose, its very essence. The Church is un-
intelligible except in relation to the Kingdom; to define this
relation is to define the Church itself.[7]

These unequivocal remarks of an eminent exegete command
attention. Between the Kingdom of God and the Church there
exists, a strong, dynamic bond, a vital relationship. The Kingdom
of God is the completion of the Church, and the Church is the
inauguration of the Kingdom. This is a fundamental datum of
christian ecclesiology. The Constitution *Lumen Gentium* says as
much when it declares that the Church is "the initial budding
forth of that kingdom. While it slowly grows, the Church strains
toward the completed Kingdom and, with all its strength, hopes
and desires to be united with its King" (no. 5).

Though we know neither the day nor the hour, it seems that
at the present time God is beckoning us to move a degree closer
to the end-time of history. The Church is apparently the object
of a grace urging her to go steadily forward toward the Kingdom.
We are, in a manner of speaking, living a καιρός, "a privileged
and opportune moment." For the Church such a moment can only
spell progress in her transformation into the Kingdom of God.

The Kingdom of God, however, is less "institutional" than
the Church, than the People of God still journeying toward the
Kingdom, generation after generation. In the Kingdom we shall
not find the visible structure of the Church, nor professions of

---

7. L. Cerfaux, "L'Église et le Règne de Dieu," *Recueil Lucien Cerfaux,*
vol. II, p. 386.

faith, nor sacraments and hierarchical ministries: these things are transitional. Consequently, living an ecclesial κχιϱός — drawing nearer to the Kingdom, qualitatively — means to advance toward more charity and more theological existence, while at the same time withdrawing in some degree from what is transitional in the ecclesiastical institution. This suggests that a crisis in regard to the "institutional" elements of the Church can mean two different things. It could mean a decline of faith and christian vitality. But it might also indicate an advance toward the fullness of the Kingdom of God.

What is to decide whether withdrawing or retreating, in some degree, from institutional features of the Church represents a deterioration of Christianity or an improvement? Obviously, some criterion is necessary, and we believe it can be found in the very purpose of the Church. In other words, wherever the christian community is growing in knowledge and appreciation of the true God, growing in charity and truth and justice, in moral integrity and christian joy; wherever, that is, the community of Christians is growing in resemblance to the eschatological community, any crisis in the "institutional" realm that may be brought on by such a development does not necessarily indicate a worsening of the community. Sometimes, as a matter of fact, it could be a sign of progress and improvement. On the other hand, whenever things are moving in the opposite direction, and the christian community is less and less the image of the eschatological community, we must not delude ourselves. The community is pale and sickly. Faith has lost its vitality. Decline prevails.

But whatever the drift of the christian community, of one thing we can be sure. We are not yet in heaven. We are still in the time of the Church, and it is still too early to dispense with everything "transitional." The believer is not yet the confirmed elect, nor the Church the ripened Kingdom.